PA PROPHETIC LENS

PAUL'S JOURNEY TO
FAITH-RIGHTEOUSNESS THROUGH
THE LAW AND PROPHETS

CLINT BYARS

Paul's Prophetic Lens: Paul's Journey to
Faith-Righteousness through
the Law and Prophets

Copyright © 2024 Clint Byars. All rights reserved.

Clint Byars

Clint Byars
Forward Ministries
3500 GA 34, Suite 15, Sharpsburg, GA 30277
USA
770-828-5826 | www.clintbyars.com

Scripture Citations:
Scripture quotations marked (NIV) are taken from the Holy Bible, New International Version®, NIV®. Copyright © 1973, 1978, 1984, 2011 by Biblica, Inc.™ Used by permission of Zondervan. All rights reserved worldwide. www. zondervan.com

Scripture quotations marked (KJV) are taken from the Holy Bible, King James Version, public domain.

INTRODUCTION

When Jesus appeared to His disciples after His resurrection, He made a profound declaration about the fulfillment of the Scriptures. In Luke 24:44-48, He explained to them that everything written about Him in the Law of Moses, the Prophets, and the Psalms must be fulfilled. Jesus opened their minds to understand the Scriptures, showing them how His suffering, death, and resurrection were foretold and necessary for the salvation of humanity. This divine revelation transformed their understanding of the Old Testament, illuminating the scriptures in a new light that pointed directly to Christ as the culmination of God's redemptive plan.

Similarly, Paul experienced a profound revelation from Christ that reshaped his understanding of the Scriptures. As a devout Pharisee, Paul was deeply knowledgeable in the Hebrew Scriptures. However, it was on the road to Damascus that Paul encountered the risen Christ and began to see the scriptures in a radically new way. In Galatians 1:11-12, Paul emphasizes that the gospel he preached was not of human origin but was received through a revelation of Jesus Christ. This revelation was not an entirely new doctrine detached from the Jewish scriptures but rather a divine illumination that revealed the hidden truths within them.

Paul's epistles reflect this profound transformation. He frequently shows how the Old Testament points to Christ and the concept of faith-righteousness. For instance, in Romans 3:21-22, Paul declares that the righteousness of God has been revealed apart from the law, to which the Law and the Prophets testify. He interprets the story of Abraham's faith in Genesis as a prototype of the faith-righteousness available to all through Christ (Romans 4). In his letters, Paul weaves together the narratives, prophecies, and laws of the Old Testament, demonstrating how they all converge in Jesus Christ. This understanding was not just an intellectual exercise but a Spirit-led revelation that unveiled the mystery of Christ as the fulfillment of God's promises.

Thus, just as Jesus opened the minds of His disciples to understand the Scriptures, He did the same for Paul. Paul's deep dive into the Hebrew Scriptures, now seen through the lens of Christ's revelation, unveiled the grand narrative of God's plan for salvation. The mystery that had been concealed for ages was now revealed: that through Jesus Christ, both Jews and Gentiles could be reconciled to God and each other, forming one body of believers justified by faith. This profound insight became the cornerstone of Paul's ministry and the message he tirelessly preached to the nations.

Romans 1:1 Paul, a bondservant of Jesus Christ, called *to be* an apostle, separated to the gospel of God **2** which He promised before through His prophets in the Holy Scriptures, **3** concerning His Son Jesus Christ our Lord, who was born of the seed of David according to the flesh, **4** *and* declared *to be* the Son of God with power according to the Spirit of holiness, by the resurrection from the dead. **5** Through Him we have received grace and apostleship for obedience to the faith among all nations for His name, **6** among whom you also are the called of Jesus Christ;

I have laid this material out as a course rather than book chapters. You are welcome to use this material to teach in your discipleship sphere, adding to each section what is appropriate for your audience or congregation.

The goal is to help people become rooted in the simple yet profound truth that... IT'S ALL ABOUT JESUS!!

DISCOVERING THE DEPTH OF PAUL'S TEACHINGS!

Join me for an enlightening journey through Paul's revelation of Jesus as the Lamb of God and the powerful truth of Faith Righteousness.

What You'll Learn:

- **Paul's Background & Scriptural Foundation**: Explore Paul's life as a Pharisee and his profound knowledge of the Old Testament.
- **The Sacrificial System & Promise of a Redeemer**: Understand how the Old Testament sacrifices point to Jesus as the ultimate Lamb of God.
- **Jesus as the Fulfillment of the Old Testament**: See how Jesus completes the Law and the Prophets through His life, death, and resurrection.
- **Paul's Teachings on Faith Righteousness**: Dive into Paul's revelation on justification by faith and its transformative power.

- **Paul's Epistles**: Study Romans, Galatians, and Hebrews to see how Paul expounded on these truths to the early church.
- **Practical Applications for Today**: Learn how to live out your faith, understand your identity in Christ, and apply Old Testament teachings in light of Christ's fulfillment.

Why This Course?

- **Deepen Your Faith**: Gain a richer, more profound understanding of the scriptures.
- **Practical Insights**: Learn how to apply biblical truths to your everyday life.
- **Community Learning**: Engage with a community of learners, sharing insights and growing together.

This course aims to provide an understanding of how Paul's revelation of Jesus as the Lamb of God and the concept of faith righteousness is deeply rooted in his study of the Old Testament scriptures. Through this structured approach, participants will gain a deeper appreciation of the continuity and fulfillment of God's plan of salvation through Jesus Christ.

TABLE OF CONTENTS

- **Overview**
  - ○ Purpose of the course
  - ○ Importance of understanding Paul's revelation
  - ○ The connection between Paul's teachings and the Old Testament

- **Lesson 1.1: Paul's Background**
  - ○ Paul's early life and education
  - ○ His status as a Pharisee and knowledge of the Law
- **Lesson 1.2: Scriptural Foundations of Paul's Revelation**

COURSE INTRODUCTION

Welcome! I'm delighted to have you join me on this journey through the scriptures, as we explore the profound insights of the Apostle Paul. This course will explore how Paul's revelation of Jesus Christ is deeply rooted in the Old Testament, showing that his teachings were not entirely new doctrines but a fulfillment of God's long-standing promises and revelations.

Let's begin by setting the stage with a bit of background. The Apostle Paul, originally known as Saul of Tarsus, was a well-educated Pharisee. He describes himself in Philippians 3:5-6 as "circumcised on the eighth day, of the people of Israel, of the tribe of Benjamin, a Hebrew of Hebrews; in regard to the law, a Pharisee; as for zeal, persecuting the church; as for righteousness based on the law, faultless."

Paul's extensive knowledge of the Jewish scriptures and his fervent adherence to the law uniquely positioned him to understand and interpret the fulfillment of these scriptures in Jesus Christ. His dramatic conversion on the road to Damascus marked the beginning of a profound shift in his understanding (Acts 9). This course aims to trace how Paul's deep study of the Old Testament scriptures led him to the revelation of Jesus as the promised Messiah and the Lamb of God who takes away the sin of the world.

In this course, we will explore several key themes:

1. **Paul's Background and Scriptural Foundation**: We'll look at Paul's early life, his education, and his deep-rooted knowledge of the Jewish scriptures.

2. **The Sacrificial System and the Promise of a Redeemer**: We'll examine the Old Testament sacrificial system and how it pointed to the need for a perfect sacrifice, which Paul recognized in Jesus.

3. **Jesus as the Fulfillment of the Old Testament**: We'll discuss how Jesus himself taught that he was the fulfillment of the Law and the Prophets and how Paul unpacked these truths.

4. **Paul's Revelation and Teachings on Faith Righteousness**: We'll delve into Paul's

teachings on justification by faith, contrasting it with the righteousness based on the law.

5. **Paul's Exposition of the Scriptures in His Epistles**: We'll study how Paul used the Old Testament scriptures in his letters to the early churches to explain and defend the gospel.

6. **Practical Applications for Believers Today**: Finally, we'll consider how Paul's revelations apply to us today and how we can live out these truths in our daily lives.

Our journey will take us through a comprehensive study of Paul's writings, especially his letters to the Romans and the Galatians, and we'll see how he consistently pointed back to the Old Testament to substantiate his teachings. We'll also look at the broader context of the sacrificial system, God's covenant with Abraham, and the prophetic writings that all pointed to Jesus as the ultimate fulfillment.

By the end of this course, you will have a deeper understanding of how Paul's revelation of Jesus as the Lamb of God was not an isolated event but a continuation and fulfillment of God's redemptive plan as revealed in the scriptures. You will also gain practical insights into how to apply these truths in your own faith journey.

Module 1:

Paul's Background and Scriptural Foundation

Welcome to Module 1 of our course. In this first module, we will lay the groundwork for understanding Paul's profound insights by exploring his background and the scriptural foundation that informed his teachings.

To fully appreciate the depth of Paul's revelation, it is essential to understand who Paul was before his encounter with Christ. As we delve into his early life, we will see that Paul, known initially as Saul of Tarsus, was not just any Jew but a Pharisee of Pharisees. He was a man deeply rooted in the Jewish tradition, well-versed in the scriptures, and zealous for the law.

In Philippians 3:5-6, Paul gives us a glimpse of his pedigree and commitment to Judaism: "circumcised on the eighth day, of the people of Israel, of the tribe of Benjamin, a Hebrew of Hebrews; in regard to the law, a Pharisee; as for zeal, persecuting the church; as for righteousness based on the law, faultless." This background is crucial because it shows that Paul's knowledge and practice of the Jewish faith were extensive and devout.

In this module, we will explore two main areas:

1. Paul's Background

o We will delve into Paul's upbringing, his education under Gamaliel, one of the most respected teachers of the law, and his early zeal in persecuting the followers of Jesus. Understanding this context helps us see the dramatic transformation that occurred in Paul's life.

2. Scriptural Foundations of Paul's Revelation

o We will examine the key Old Testament scriptures that Paul knew intimately. This includes the Law (Torah), the Prophets (Nevi'im), and the Writings (Ketuvim). Paul's deep study of these texts laid the foundation for his later revelations and teachings.

By understanding Paul's background and scriptural foundation, we can better grasp how his profound revelation of Jesus as the Lamb of God and the concept of faith righteousness were not isolated ideas but deeply rooted in the scriptures he had studied and revered all his life. Paul's teachings were a continuation and fulfillment of the divine narrative that God had been unfolding through the ages.

As we journey through this module, we will see how Paul's rigorous training in the scriptures and his passionate commitment to the law provided the framework for his later teachings. We will explore specific Old Testament passages that were pivotal in shaping Paul's understanding and how these scriptures pointed to the coming of the Messiah, whom Paul recognized in Jesus Christ.

Let's begin by diving into the life of Saul of Tarsus, exploring his formative years, his education, and his initial zeal for the law. This will set the stage for understanding the profound transformation that occurred on the road to Damascus and how Paul's deep scriptural foundation prepared him to receive and articulate the revelation of Jesus as the fulfillment of God's promises.

LESSON 1.1: PAUL'S BACKGROUND

Welcome to Lesson 1.1 of our course, "Paul's Revelation of Jesus as the Lamb of God and Faith Righteousness Rooted in Scripture." In this lesson, we will delve into the background of the Apostle Paul, known initially as Saul of Tarsus. Understanding Paul's early life, his education, and his fervent commitment to Judaism is crucial to appreciating the depth of his later revelations about Jesus Christ.

Let's start by looking at Paul's early life. Saul was born in Tarsus, a city in the region of Cilicia, which is in modern-day Turkey. Tarsus was an important city known for its culture and learning, which meant that Saul had access to a rich educational environment from a young age.

In Acts 22:3, Paul himself provides us with some insights into his background. He states, "I am a Jew, born in Tarsus of Cilicia, but brought up in this city. I studied under Gamaliel and was thoroughly trained in the law of our ancestors. I was just as zealous for God as any of you are today." This verse highlights several important points:

1. **Jewish Heritage:** Saul was a Jew by birth, emphasizing his ethnic and religious identity.

2. **Education in Jerusalem:** Although born in Tarsus, Saul was brought up in Jerusalem, the heart of Jewish religious life.

3. **Training under Gamaliel:** Gamaliel was a highly respected Pharisee and teacher of the law. Being a student of Gamaliel meant that Saul received an excellent education in the Jewish scriptures and traditions.

4. **Zeal for the Law:** Saul's zeal for God and the law was a defining characteristic of his early life.

Let's expand on these points. Saul's upbringing in a Jewish family in Tarsus would have given him a strong foundation in the Hebrew scriptures. His move to Jerusalem for further education under Gamaliel signifies a deepening of his commitment to the Jewish faith and traditions. Gamaliel was known for his wisdom and balanced approach to the law, and Saul's training under him would have been rigorous and comprehensive.

In Philippians 3:5-6, Paul provides further details about his background: "circumcised on the eighth day, of the people of Israel, of the tribe of Benjamin, a Hebrew of Hebrews; in regard to the law, a Pharisee; as for zeal, persecuting the church; as for righteousness based on the law, faultless." This passage highlights several key aspects of Saul's identity and credentials:

1. **Circumcised on the Eighth Day:** This indicates his adherence to the Jewish law from birth.

2. **Tribe of Benjamin:** Saul was from a distinguished tribe within Israel, adding to his sense of identity and pride.

3. **Hebrew of Hebrews:** He was deeply rooted in his Jewish heritage and traditions.

4. **Pharisee:** As a Pharisee, Saul belonged to a group known for their strict observance of the law and traditions.

5. **Zeal and Righteousness:** His zeal for persecuting the early church and his claim of being faultless in legal righteousness highlight his fervent commitment to Judaism.

Saul's zeal for the law was evident in his actions. In Acts 8:3, we read that "Saul began to destroy the church. Going from house to house, he dragged off both men and women and put them in prison." His zeal led him to actively persecute the early followers of Jesus, believing that he was upholding the purity of the Jewish faith.

Saul's encounter with Jesus on the road to Damascus was a turning point in his life. This dramatic conversion is recorded in Acts 9. Saul was on his way to Damascus to arrest followers of Jesus when he was struck by a bright light and heard the voice of Jesus asking, "Saul, Saul, why do you persecute me?" This encounter left Saul blind for three days until Ananias, a disciple of Jesus, laid hands on him and he regained his sight.

Following his conversion, Saul, now known as Paul, began to preach that Jesus is the Son of God. This radical transformation from a persecutor of Christians to a proclaimer of Christ is one of the most powerful testimonies of the gospel's transformative power.

To summarize, Paul's background as a well-educated Pharisee and his zealous commitment to the Jewish law provided a strong foundation for his later teachings. His deep understanding of the scriptures and his training under Gamaliel equipped him to interpret the Old Testament in the light of his revelation of Jesus Christ. This background helps us appreciate the depth and richness of Paul's teachings on faith righteousness and the fulfillment of God's promises in Jesus.

In our next lesson, we will explore the specific scriptural foundations that Paul drew upon to develop his revelation of Jesus as the Lamb of God and the righteousness that comes by faith.

LESSON 1.2: SCRIPTURAL FOUNDATIONS OF PAUL'S REVELATION

Welcome to Lesson 1.2 of our course, "Paul's Revelation of Jesus as the Lamb of God and Faith Righteousness Rooted in Scripture." In this lesson, we will explore the scriptural foundations that deeply influenced Paul's revelation of Jesus Christ. By understanding these foundations, we can see how Paul's teachings were firmly rooted in the Old Testament scriptures he had studied so extensively.

Let's begin by considering the Jewish scriptures, which are divided into three main sections: the Law (Torah), the Prophets (Nevi'im), and the Writings (Ketuvim). These texts were central to the religious life and identity of the Jewish people, and Paul, as a Pharisee, would have been thoroughly versed in them.

First, let's look at the **Law**, or **Torah**, which consists of the first five books of the Bible: Genesis, Exodus, Leviticus, Numbers, and Deuteronomy. These books contain the creation narrative, the history of the patriarchs, the Exodus from Egypt, the giving of the Law at Mount Sinai, and the early history of Israel. Several key themes and events in the Torah are critical to understanding Paul's later revelations:

1. **The Promise to Abraham**: In Genesis 12:1-3, God calls Abraham and promises to make him into a great nation and to bless all the families of the earth through him. This promise is foundational to the understanding of God's redemptive plan for humanity.

2. **The Covenant and the Law**: In Exodus 19-20, God establishes a covenant with Israel at Mount Sinai and gives them the Ten Commandments. This covenant relationship and the giving of the Law are central to Jewish identity and practice.

3. **The Sacrificial System**: The book of Leviticus outlines the various sacrifices and offerings required by the Law. These sacrifices were a means for atonement and maintaining a right relationship with God, foreshadowing the ultimate sacrifice of Jesus Christ.

Next, let's examine the **Prophets**. The Prophets include both the Former Prophets (historical books like Joshua, Judges, Samuel, and Kings) and the Latter Prophets (Isaiah, Jeremiah, Ezekiel, and the Twelve Minor Prophets). These books contain God's messages to His people through His prophets, calling them to repentance and foretelling future events. Key prophetic themes include:

1. **Messianic Prophecies**: Many prophecies in the books of the Prophets point to the coming of a Messiah. For example, Isaiah 53 speaks of the suffering servant who would bear the sins of many, a passage that Paul would later interpret as referring to Jesus Christ.

2. **The New Covenant**: In Jeremiah 31:31-34, God promises a new covenant with His people, one that involves writing His law on their hearts. This concept of a new covenant is pivotal in Paul's teachings on the transformative power of the gospel.

Lastly, we have the **Writings**, which include books like Psalms, Proverbs, Job, and Daniel. These texts provide wisdom, poetry, and apocalyptic visions. Some significant elements from the Writings that Paul would have drawn upon include:

1. **The Psalms**: Many Psalms contain Messianic themes and prophecies. For example, Psalm 22 vividly describes the suffering of a righteous one, which Jesus quotes on the cross, indicating its fulfillment in Him.

2. **Wisdom Literature**: Books like Proverbs and Ecclesiastes offer insights into righteous living and the human condition, themes that resonate with Paul's teachings on practical Christian living.

Now, let's consider how Paul used these scriptures to develop his revelation of Jesus as the Lamb of God and the concept of faith righteousness.

One of the central themes in Paul's revelation is the idea of justification by faith, rather than by works of the law. This concept is rooted in the story of Abraham. In Genesis 15:6, it says, "Abram believed the LORD, and he credited it to him as righteousness." Paul refers to this passage in Romans 4 and Galatians 3 to argue that righteousness comes through faith, not through adherence to the law.

Paul also draws heavily on the sacrificial system outlined in Leviticus to explain Jesus' role as the ultimate sacrifice. In Romans 3:25, Paul writes, "God presented Christ as a sacrifice of atonement, through the shedding of his blood—to be received by faith." This language of sacrifice and atonement is directly connected to the Old Testament sacrificial system.

Paul's understanding of Jesus as the fulfillment of the Messianic prophecies is evident in his letters. For instance, in 1 Corinthians 15:3-4, Paul states, "For what

I received I passed on to you as of first importance: that Christ died for our sins according to the Scriptures, that he was buried, that he was raised on the third day according to the Scriptures." Here, Paul emphasizes that Jesus' death and resurrection were in accordance with the scriptures, demonstrating their fulfillment in Him.

Paul's revelation of Jesus as the Lamb of God and the concept of faith righteousness were deeply rooted in the Old Testament scriptures he had studied. The promises to Abraham, the sacrificial system, the prophecies of a coming Messiah, and the wisdom literature all provided a rich foundation for Paul's teachings. By understanding these scriptural foundations, we can appreciate the continuity of God's redemptive plan and how Paul's teachings are a fulfillment of the scriptures.

In our next module, we will explore the sacrificial system in greater detail and see how it points to the need for a perfect sacrifice, which Paul recognized in Jesus Christ.

MODULE 2:

THE SACRIFICIAL SYSTEM AND THE PROMISE OF A REDEEMER

Welcome to Module 2. In this module, we will delve into the sacrificial system outlined in the Old Testament and explore how it foreshadowed the need for a perfect sacrifice—a need that Paul recognized as being fulfilled in Jesus Christ.

To fully understand Paul's revelation of Jesus as the Lamb of God, it is crucial to grasp the significance of the sacrificial system established in the Law of Moses. This system was central to the worship and religious life of Israel. It provided a means for atonement, forgiveness, and maintaining a covenant relationship with God. The sacrificial system was not an end in itself but pointed forward to a greater reality and a more perfect sacrifice.

In this module, we will explore two main themes:

1. The Sacrificial System in the Old Testament

- o We will examine the various types of sacrifices described in the book of Leviticus, including burnt offerings, sin offerings, and peace offerings. Each type of sacrifice had specific purposes and symbolized different aspects of atonement and reconciliation with God.

- o We will look at the Day of Atonement (Yom Kippur), the most significant day in the Jewish calendar, where the high priest made a yearly atonement for the sins of the people. This annual ritual pointed to the need for a once-for-all sacrifice, which Paul identified in Jesus.

2. The Promise of a Redeemer

- o We will explore the story of Abraham and Isaac in Genesis 22, where God provides a ram as a substitute sacrifice for Isaac. This story is a powerful foreshadowing of God's ultimate provision of a substitute—Jesus Christ, the Lamb of God.

o We will consider the prophetic promises of a coming Redeemer, particularly those found in Isaiah and the Psalms, and how these prophecies set the stage for the coming of Jesus.

The sacrificial system taught the Israelites several important theological truths:

- **The Seriousness of Sin:** Sin was not a trivial matter; it required a blood sacrifice for atonement.
- **The Holiness of God:** God's holiness demanded that sin be dealt with justly.
- **The Need for a Substitute:** The sacrificial animals served as substitutes, bearing the punishment that the people deserved.

Paul, as a Pharisee, would have been intimately familiar with these aspects of the sacrificial system. After his revelation of Jesus on the road to Damascus, Paul came to understand that the sacrificial system was a shadow of the greater reality found in Christ. In Hebrews 10:1, we read, "The law is only a shadow of the good things that are coming—not the realities themselves." Paul saw Jesus as the fulfillment of the sacrificial system, the ultimate Lamb of God who takes away the sin of the world (John 1:29).

By understanding the sacrificial system and its significance, we can better appreciate Paul's teachings on the atonement and the righteousness that comes by faith in Jesus Christ. This module will help us see how the Old Testament sacrificial system and the promise of a Redeemer point directly to Jesus and how Paul's revelation was deeply rooted in these scriptural truths.

As we journey through this module, we will uncover the profound connections between the sacrifices of the Old Testament and the sacrifice of Jesus Christ. We will see how the story of Abraham and Isaac foreshadows God's provision of His own Son as the ultimate sacrifice. We will also explore the prophetic promises of a Redeemer who would bring true and lasting atonement.

Let's begin by diving into the details of the Old Testament sacrificial system and understanding its various components and purposes. This foundation will set the stage for recognizing the fulfillment of these sacrifices in Jesus Christ, as Paul so powerfully articulated in his writings.

LESSON 2.1: THE SACRIFICIAL SYSTEM IN THE OLD TESTAMENT

Welcome to Lesson 2.1. In this lesson, we will delve into the sacrificial system outlined in the Old Testament, particularly in the book of Leviticus. Understanding this system is crucial for appreciating how Paul viewed Jesus as the ultimate sacrifice that fulfills and transcends the Old Testament sacrifices.

Let's start by exploring the various types of sacrifices described in Leviticus. The sacrificial system was central to the religious life of Israel, providing a means for atonement, reconciliation with God, and maintaining the covenant relationship.

There were several types of sacrifices, each with its specific purpose and significance:

1. **Burnt Offerings (Leviticus 1)**
   o **Purpose**: The burnt offering was made to atone for the worshiper's sins and express their devotion to God. The entire animal, except the skin, was burned on the altar.
   o **Significance**: The complete burning of the offering symbolized the worshiper's total surrender to God. It also pointed to the need for a perfect, unblemished sacrifice, which Paul later identified in Jesus Christ.

2. **Grain Offerings (Leviticus 2)**
   - **Purpose**: The grain offering was a tribute to God, recognizing His provision and expressing gratitude. It consisted of fine flour, olive oil, and incense.
   - **Significance**: This offering symbolized the dedication of one's labor and produce to God. It highlighted the importance of giving thanks and acknowledging God's blessings.

3. **Peace Offerings (Leviticus 3)**
   - **Purpose**: The peace offering, also known as the fellowship offering, was made to express gratitude and establish fellowship with God. Parts of the animal were burned, while the rest was eaten in a communal meal.
   - **Significance**: This offering represented peace and communion with God. It foreshadowed the ultimate reconciliation and fellowship with God through Jesus Christ.

4. **Sin Offerings (Leviticus 4)**
   - **Purpose**: The sin offering was made to atone for unintentional sins and cleanse the worshiper from impurity. The blood of the

animal was sprinkled on the altar and other sacred objects.

- o **Significance**: This offering emphasized the seriousness of sin and the need for purification. It pointed to the ultimate purification and forgiveness of sins through Jesus' sacrifice.

5. **Guilt Offerings (Leviticus 5)**

- o **Purpose**: The guilt offering, or trespass offering, was made to atone for specific sins, particularly those involving desecration of holy things or deception. The worshiper also had to make restitution.

- o **Significance**: This offering underscored the need for repentance and restitution. It highlighted the need for a comprehensive atonement, which Paul saw fulfilled in Christ.

Now, let's take a closer look at the **Day of Atonement (Yom Kippur)**, the most significant day in the Jewish calendar. This annual ritual is described in Leviticus 16 and involved several key elements:

1. **High Priest's Role**: Only the high priest could perform the rituals on the Day of Atonement.

He would enter the Most Holy Place (Holy of Holies) to make atonement for himself and the people.

2. **Sacrifices**: The high priest would sacrifice a bull for his own sins and a goat for the sins of the people. The blood of these animals was sprinkled on the atonement cover of the Ark of the Covenant.

3. **Scapegoat**: A second goat, called the scapegoat, was chosen. The high priest would lay his hands on the scapegoat's head, confessing the sins of the people, and then send it into the wilderness, symbolizing the removal of their sins.

The Day of Atonement illustrated several important theological truths:

- **The Need for Atonement**: The ritual emphasized the necessity of atonement for sin to maintain a relationship with God.
- **The Role of the High Priest**: The high priest acted as a mediator between God and the people, foreshadowing Jesus' role as our High Priest.
- **The Symbolism of the Scapegoat**: The scapegoat symbolized the removal of sin,

pointing to Jesus' role in taking away the sins of the world.

Paul, in his epistles, draws on the imagery and significance of these sacrifices to explain the atoning work of Jesus Christ. For example, in Romans 3:25, Paul writes, "God presented Christ as a sacrifice of atonement, through the shedding of his blood—to be received by faith." Here, Paul directly connects Jesus' sacrifice to the concept of atonement established in the Old Testament sacrificial system.

Additionally, in Hebrews 9:11-14, we read, "But when Christ came as high priest of the good things that are now already here, he went through the greater and more perfect tabernacle that is not made with human hands... He did not enter by means of the blood of goats and calves; but he entered the Most Holy Place once for all by his own blood, thus obtaining eternal redemption." This passage highlights how Jesus, as the ultimate High Priest, entered the heavenly sanctuary and offered His own blood, securing eternal redemption for us.

To summarize, the Old Testament sacrificial system was a vital part of Israel's worship and relationship with God. It taught important truths about sin, atonement, and reconciliation. Paul's deep understanding of this system allowed him to see and proclaim Jesus as the fulfillment of these sacrifices—the perfect Lamb of God who takes away the sin of the world.

In our next lesson, we will explore the promise of a Redeemer, particularly focusing on the story of Abraham and Isaac and the prophetic promises of the Messiah.

LESSON 2.2: ABRAHAM AND THE PROMISE OF A LAMB

In this lesson, we will explore the story of Abraham and Isaac in Genesis 22 and the prophetic promises of a Redeemer. Understanding these key narratives helps us see how Paul's revelation of Jesus as the Lamb of God was deeply rooted in the scriptures.

Let's begin with the story of Abraham and Isaac. In Genesis 22:1-19, we read about a profound test of faith that Abraham experienced. God commanded Abraham to take his beloved son Isaac to the region of Moriah and sacrifice him as a burnt offering on one of the mountains. This command was both shocking and perplexing, given that Isaac was the son of promise through whom God had said He would establish His covenant.

Let's read the key portions of this passage to understand its significance. Genesis 22:1-2 says, "Some time later God tested Abraham. He said to him, 'Abraham!' 'Here I am,' he replied. Then God said, 'Take your son, your only son, whom you love—Isaac—

and go to the region of Moriah. Sacrifice him there as a burnt offering on a mountain I will show you.'"

Abraham's obedience is immediate and unwavering. He sets out early the next morning with Isaac and two servants, carrying wood for the burnt offering. As they approach the mountain, Abraham instructs his servants to stay behind, saying in verse 5, "Stay here with the donkey while I and the boy go over there. We will worship and then we will come back to you."

Notice Abraham's faith in God's promise. He tells his servants that both he and Isaac will return, indicating his belief that God would somehow fulfill His promise regarding Isaac. As they ascend the mountain, Isaac notices the absence of a sacrificial animal and asks his father, "The fire and wood are here, but where is the lamb for the burnt offering?" Abraham's response in verse 8 is profound: "God himself will provide the lamb for the burnt offering, my son."

This statement of faith is pivotal. Abraham believed that God would provide the necessary sacrifice. When they reached the place God had indicated, Abraham built an altar, arranged the wood, and bound Isaac. Just as he was about to slay his son, the angel of the Lord called out to him from heaven, "Do not lay a hand on the boy... Now I know that you fear God, because you

have not withheld from me your son, your only son"
(Genesis 22:12).

At that moment, Abraham looked up and saw a
ram caught by its horns in a thicket. He took the ram
and sacrificed it as a burnt offering instead of his son.
In verse 14, we read, "So Abraham called that place
The Lord Will Provide. And to this day it is said, 'On
the mountain of the Lord it will be provided.'"

This story is rich with prophetic symbolism and
theological significance. Let's highlight a few key points:

1. **Foreshadowing of Christ**: Isaac's role as the
   beloved son who carries the wood for his own
   sacrifice foreshadows Jesus, the beloved Son of
   God, who carried His cross to Golgotha.
2. **Substitutionary Sacrifice**: The ram
   provided by God as a substitute for Isaac points
   to Jesus as the ultimate substitute, the Lamb of
   God who takes away the sin of the world.
3. **Faith and Obedience**: Abraham's faith
   and obedience highlight the importance of
   trusting God's promises, even when they seem
   impossible.

The promise of a Redeemer is further elaborated
in the prophetic books of the Old Testament. Let's
look at some key Messianic prophecies:

1. **Isaiah 53:3-7**: This passage, often referred to as the Suffering Servant, describes the Messiah as one who is "despised and rejected by mankind, a man of suffering, and familiar with pain... But he was pierced for our transgressions, he was crushed for our iniquities; the punishment that brought us peace was on him, and by his wounds we are healed." This vivid description of the suffering and sacrificial death of the Messiah directly points to Jesus' crucifixion.

2. **Psalm 22**: This psalm contains striking parallels to the crucifixion of Jesus. Verses 16-18 say, "Dogs surround me, a pack of villains encircles me; they pierce my hands and my feet. All my bones are on display; people stare and gloat over me. They divide my clothes among them and cast lots for my garment." These details were fulfilled in Jesus' suffering and death on the cross.

3. **Micah 5:2**: This prophecy indicates the birthplace of the Messiah: "But you, Bethlehem Ephrathah, though you are small among the clans of Judah, out of you will come for me one who will be ruler over Israel, whose origins are from of old, from ancient times." Jesus' birth in Bethlehem fulfills this prophecy.

Paul, with his profound knowledge of the scriptures, recognized Jesus as the fulfillment of these prophecies. In Galatians 3:16, Paul writes, "The promises were spoken to Abraham and to his seed. Scripture does not say 'and to seeds,' meaning many people, but 'and to your seed,' meaning one person, who is Christ." Paul understood that the promise of a Redeemer was ultimately fulfilled in Jesus Christ.

Furthermore, Paul's revelation of Jesus as the Lamb of God is deeply connected to these scriptural foundations. In 1 Corinthians 5:7, Paul writes, "For Christ, our Passover lamb, has been sacrificed." Here, Paul explicitly identifies Jesus with the Passover lamb, whose blood protected the Israelites from the angel of death in Egypt, symbolizing deliverance and redemption.

To summarize, the story of Abraham and Isaac, along with the Messianic prophecies, provided a rich foundation for understanding Jesus as the promised Redeemer and the ultimate sacrificial Lamb. Paul's deep study of these scriptures allowed him to see and proclaim Jesus as the fulfillment of God's redemptive plan.

In our next module, we will explore how Jesus himself taught that he was the fulfillment of the Law and the Prophets and how Paul unpacked these truths in his teachings.

MODULE 3:

JESUS AS THE FULFILLMENT OF THE OLD TESTAMENT

In this module, we will explore how Jesus Christ is the fulfillment of the Old Testament. Understanding this concept is crucial for appreciating Paul's teachings and seeing the continuity of God's redemptive plan throughout the scriptures.

The central theme of this module is the fulfillment of the Law and the Prophets in the person and work of Jesus Christ. Jesus himself made bold claims about fulfilling the Old Testament scriptures. In Matthew 5:17, He said, "Do not think that I have come to abolish the Law or the Prophets; I have not come to abolish them but to fulfill them." This statement sets the stage for understanding how Jesus viewed His mission and how Paul later interpreted these events.

In this module, we will explore three main themes:

1. Prophecies of the Messiah

o   We will delve into key Messianic prophecies from the Old Testament and see how they pointed to the coming of Jesus Christ. These prophecies include those found in Isaiah, Psalms, Micah, and other books. We will see how Jesus fulfilled these specific predictions, affirming His identity as the promised Messiah.

2. Jesus' Own Teachings on the Fulfillment of the Law and Prophets

o   We will examine Jesus' teachings and statements about fulfilling the scriptures. This includes His declaration in Matthew 5:17-18 and His post-resurrection teaching to the disciples on the road to Emmaus, where He explained how the Law, the Prophets, and the Psalms spoke about Him (Luke 24:27, 44-45).

3. Paul's Understanding of Jesus as the Fulfillment of the Scriptures

o We will explore how Paul, in his epistles, articulated the fulfillment of the Old Testament in Jesus. Paul's deep understanding of the scriptures and his revelation of Jesus as the Messiah allowed him to connect the dots and show the early Christian communities how Jesus was the fulfillment of God's promises.

By understanding how Jesus fulfills the Old Testament, we gain a deeper appreciation of the continuity and coherence of the biblical narrative. This perspective helps us see that the New Testament is not a departure from the Old Testament but rather its culmination and completion in Christ.

Jesus' life, death, and resurrection were not random events but the fulfillment of a divine plan set in motion from the very beginning. The prophecies and promises of the Old Testament find their "yes" in Him (2 Corinthians 1:20). This fulfillment brings clarity to the purpose of the Law, the sacrificial system, and the prophetic messages, all of which point to Jesus as the ultimate solution to humanity's sin problem.

As we journey through this module, we will uncover the rich tapestry of Old Testament prophecies and see how Jesus' life and ministry perfectly align with God's redemptive plan. We will also explore how Paul, with his extensive knowledge of the scriptures, understood and taught these truths to the early church.

Let's begin by diving into the prophecies of the Messiah and see how they set the stage for the coming of Jesus Christ.

LESSON 3.1: PROPHECIES OF THE MESSIAH

In this lesson, we will delve into key Messianic prophecies from the Old Testament and explore how they pointed to the coming of Jesus Christ. Understanding these prophecies helps us see the continuity of God's redemptive plan and how Jesus fulfills the scriptures.

Let's start with one of the most significant Messianic prophecies found in the book of Isaiah. Isaiah 53 is often referred to as the "Suffering Servant" passage. It provides a vivid and detailed description of the Messiah's suffering and sacrificial death.

Isaiah 53:3-7:

"He was despised and rejected by mankind, a man of suffering, and familiar with pain. Like one from whom people hide their faces he was despised, and we held him in low esteem. Surely he took up our pain and bore our suffering, yet we considered

him punished by God, stricken by him, and afflicted. But he was pierced for our transgressions, he was crushed for our iniquities; the punishment that brought us peace was on him, and by his wounds we are healed. We all, like sheep, have gone astray, each of us has turned to our own way; and the Lord has laid on him the iniquity of us all. He was oppressed and afflicted, yet he did not open his mouth; he was led like a lamb to the slaughter, and as a sheep before its shearers is silent, so he did not open his mouth."

This passage clearly describes the Messiah as one who suffers on behalf of others. He is pierced for our transgressions and crushed for our iniquities. This prophecy points directly to Jesus' crucifixion, where He bore the sins of humanity on the cross. The imagery of a lamb led to the slaughter also connects to the sacrificial system we discussed in Module 2, highlighting Jesus as the ultimate sacrificial Lamb.

Another significant prophecy is found in Micah 5:2, which predicts the birthplace of the Messiah:

"But you, Bethlehem Ephrathah, though you are small among the clans of Judah, out of you will come for me one who will be ruler over Israel, whose origins are from of old, from ancient times."

This prophecy was fulfilled in Jesus' birth in Bethlehem, as recorded in the Gospels of Matthew and Luke. Despite Bethlehem's small size and seeming insignificance, it was chosen as the birthplace of the Messiah, fulfilling this ancient prophecy and demonstrating God's sovereign plan.

Let's turn to the book of Psalms. Psalm 22 is another profound Messianic prophecy that vividly describes the suffering of the Messiah. Let's read Psalm 22:16-18:

"Dogs surround me, a pack of villains encircles me; they pierce my hands and my feet. All my bones are on display; people stare and gloat over me. They divide my clothes among them and cast lots for my garment."

This psalm, written by David, contains striking parallels to the crucifixion of Jesus. The specific details of pierced hands and feet and the casting of lots for His garments were fulfilled in Jesus' crucifixion, as recorded in the Gospels. These precise fulfillments underscore the divine inspiration and accuracy of the scriptures.

Moving to Zechariah 9:9, we find a prophecy about the Messiah's entry into Jerusalem:

"Rejoice greatly, Daughter Zion! Shout, Daughter Jerusalem! See, your king comes to you, righteous and victorious, lowly and riding on a donkey, on a colt, the foal of a donkey."

This prophecy was fulfilled on Palm Sunday when Jesus entered Jerusalem riding on a donkey, as described in Matthew 21:1-11. The crowds hailed Him as the Son of David, recognizing Him as the promised King. This event fulfilled Zechariah's prophecy and signaled the coming of the Messiah in humility and peace.

Finally, let's consider the prophecy in Daniel 7:13-14, which speaks of the Messiah's eternal kingdom:

"In my vision at night I looked, and there before me was one like a son of man, coming with the clouds of heaven. He approached the Ancient of Days and was led into his presence. He was given authority, glory and sovereign power; all nations and peoples of every language worshiped him. His dominion is an everlasting dominion that will not pass away, and his kingdom is one that will never be destroyed."

Jesus often referred to Himself as the "Son of Man," directly connecting Himself to this prophecy. After His resurrection and ascension, He was given all authority and power, and His kingdom is indeed everlasting. This prophecy points to Jesus' ultimate reign and the eternal nature of His kingdom.

To summarize, the Old Testament contains numerous prophecies that point to the coming of the Messiah. These prophecies provide detailed descriptions of the Messiah's birth, suffering, death, and eternal reign. Jesus' life, ministry, death, and resurrection fulfilled these prophecies, demonstrating the continuity of God's redemptive plan.

Paul, with his extensive knowledge of the scriptures, recognized and proclaimed Jesus as the fulfillment of these Messianic prophecies. In his letters, Paul consistently pointed back to the Old Testament to show that Jesus was indeed the promised Messiah who fulfilled God's promises to His people.

In our next lesson, we will examine Jesus' own teachings on the fulfillment of the Law and the Prophets. We will explore how Jesus interpreted the scriptures and revealed that they pointed to Him.

LESSON 3.2: JESUS' OWN TEACHINGS ON THE FULFILLMENT OF THE LAW AND PROPHETS

In this lesson, we will explore how Jesus himself taught that he was the fulfillment of the Law and the Prophets. By examining Jesus' own words and actions, we can see how he viewed his mission and how it aligns with Paul's later teachings.

Let's begin with one of the most direct statements Jesus made about fulfilling the scriptures. In Matthew 5:17-18, Jesus says:

"Do not think that I have come to abolish the Law or the Prophets; I have not come to abolish them but to fulfill them. For truly I tell you, until heaven and earth disappear, not the smallest letter, not the least stroke of a pen, will by any means disappear from the Law until everything is accomplished."

Here, Jesus clearly states that his mission is not to abolish the Law or the Prophets but to fulfill them. This fulfillment means bringing them to their intended completion and purpose. Jesus embodies the perfect obedience to the Law and brings to fruition the prophetic promises about the Messiah.

Another significant teaching moment comes after Jesus' resurrection. In Luke 24:25-27, on the road to Emmaus, Jesus encounters two of his disciples who are confused and disheartened by the recent events. Jesus says to them:

"How foolish you are, and how slow to believe all that the prophets have spoken! Did not the Messiah have to suffer these things and then enter his glory?" And beginning with Moses and all the Prophets, he explained to them what was said in all the Scriptures concerning himself."

Jesus takes them through the scriptures, explaining how the Law and the Prophets pointed to his suffering and glory. This teaching moment underscores that the entire Old Testament is a testimony about Jesus. By interpreting the scriptures in this way, Jesus provides a hermeneutical key for understanding the Old Testament as ultimately pointing to him.

Later in the same chapter, Jesus appears to his disciples and reiterates this teaching. In Luke 24:44-45, he says:

"This is what I told you while I was still with you: Everything must be fulfilled that is written about me in the Law of Moses, the Prophets, and the Psalms." Then he opened their minds so they could understand the Scriptures."

Jesus emphasizes that the entirety of the Jewish scriptures—the Law, the Prophets, and the Psalms—contains prophecies and types that he fulfills. By opening their minds to understand the scriptures, Jesus enables his disciples to see how his life, death, and resurrection fulfill God's redemptive plan.

Let's look at some specific examples of how Jesus fulfills the Law and the Prophets:

1. **Fulfillment of the Law**:
    o **Moral Law**: Jesus perfectly obeys the moral law, living a sinless life. In Matthew 5-7, the Sermon on the Mount, Jesus expounds on the true meaning of the law, showing that it is not merely about external compliance but about the heart's intentions.
    o **Ceremonial Law**: Jesus fulfills the ceremonial aspects of the law through his sacrificial death. As the ultimate high priest and perfect sacrifice, he makes the old sacrificial system obsolete. Hebrews 9:11-12 states, "But when Christ came as high priest of the good things that are now already here, he went through the greater and more perfect tabernacle... He did not enter by means of the blood of goats and

calves; but he entered the Most Holy Place once for all by his own blood, thus obtaining eternal redemption."

o **Civil Law**: While the civil laws governed the nation of Israel, Jesus fulfills their underlying principles by establishing a new covenant community—the church, which transcends ethnic and national boundaries.

2. **Fulfillment of Prophecies**:

o **Messianic Prophecies**: As we discussed in the previous lesson, Jesus fulfills numerous Messianic prophecies, such as his birth in Bethlehem (Micah 5:2), his suffering and death (Isaiah 53), and his resurrection (Psalm 16:10).

o **Typology**: Jesus also fulfills various Old Testament types and shadows. For example, he is the true Passover Lamb (1 Corinthians 5:7) and the true manna from heaven (John 6:32-35).

Jesus' teachings and actions consistently demonstrate that he is the fulfillment of the Old Testament. This understanding is crucial for interpreting the scriptures and recognizing the continuity of God's redemptive plan. Jesus' fulfillment of the Law and the Prophets validates his identity as the Messiah and provides the foundation for Paul's teachings.

In the next lesson, we will explore how Paul understood and articulated Jesus as the fulfillment of the scriptures. We will see how Paul's deep knowledge of the Old Testament and his revelation of Jesus Christ allowed him to explain and defend the gospel to the early Christian communities.

MODULE 4:

PAUL'S REVELATION AND TEACHINGS ON FAITH RIGHTEOUSNESS

In this module, we will look into Paul's profound revelation and teachings on faith righteousness. Understanding Paul's perspective on justification by faith, rather than by works of the law, is essential for grasping the core message of the gospel.

After his dramatic conversion on the road to Damascus, Paul's understanding of the scriptures and his revelation of Jesus Christ underwent a radical transformation. He moved from being a zealous Pharisee, deeply committed to the law, to a passionate apostle of Jesus Christ, proclaiming the message of salvation by faith.

In this module, we will explore three main themes:

1. **Paul's Conversion and Initial Revelation**:
   o We will begin by examining Paul's conversion experience and the immediate impact it had on his understanding of Jesus and the scriptures. This foundational event was pivotal in shaping Paul's theology and mission.

2. **Justification by Faith**:
   o We will delve into Paul's teachings on justification by faith. Key passages in Romans and Galatians will be our focus as we unpack Paul's arguments that righteousness comes through faith in Jesus Christ, not by adhering to the works of the law.

3. **The Role of the Law in Revealing Sin and the Need for a Savior**:
   o We will explore Paul's perspective on the purpose of the law. Paul taught that the law serves to reveal sin and our need for a savior, leading us to Christ. Understanding this role of the law is crucial for appreciating the transformative power of the gospel.

Paul's revelation and teachings on faith righteousness were revolutionary. In a religious context that emphasized strict adherence to the law, Paul proclaimed a gospel of grace, emphasizing that righteousness and salvation are gifts received through faith in Jesus Christ. This message not only challenged the prevailing religious norms but also offered a profound hope of redemption and reconciliation with God.

Paul's letters, especially Romans and Galatians, provide a comprehensive exposition of his theology of justification by faith. In Romans 3:21-22, Paul writes:

"But now apart from the law the righteousness of God has been made known, to which the Law and the Prophets testify. This righteousness is given through faith in Jesus Christ to all who believe."

This passage encapsulates the essence of Paul's message: the righteousness of God is revealed apart from the law and is accessible to all through faith in Jesus Christ. Paul meticulously argues that this righteousness is rooted in the promises of God, as revealed in the scriptures, and fulfilled in Jesus.

Throughout this module, we will trace Paul's theological journey from his conversion to his mature reflections on faith righteousness. We will see how his deep knowledge of the Old Testament and his revelation of Jesus Christ converged to form a coherent and powerful message of salvation by faith.

As we journey through Paul's writings, we will gain a deeper understanding of how the gospel of Jesus

Christ transforms our relationship with God. We will see how Paul's teachings on faith righteousness offer a liberating and life-giving message that continues to resonate with believers today.

Let's begin by examining Paul's conversion and the immediate impact it had on his understanding of Jesus and the scriptures.

LESSON 4.1: PAUL'S CONVERSION AND INITIAL REVELATION

In this lesson, we will explore the dramatic conversion of Saul of Tarsus—later known as the Apostle Paul—and the immediate impact this event had on his understanding of Jesus and the scriptures. Paul's conversion is a foundational moment that set the stage for his profound theological insights and missionary endeavors.

Let's begin by recounting the story of Paul's conversion, as recorded in Acts 9:1-19. Saul was a zealous Pharisee, deeply committed to the Jewish law and fiercely opposed to the followers of Jesus. He sought to arrest and persecute Christians, believing he was upholding the purity of the Jewish faith.

Acts 9:1-2 sets the scene:

"Meanwhile, Saul was still breathing out murderous threats against the Lord's disciples. He went to the high priest and asked

him for letters to the synagogues in Damascus, so that if he found any there who belonged to the Way, whether men or women, he might take them as prisoners to Jerusalem."

Saul's journey to Damascus took an unexpected turn. In Acts 9:3-6, we read:

"As he neared Damascus on his journey, suddenly a light from heaven flashed around him. He fell to the ground and heard a voice say to him, 'Saul, Saul, why do you persecute me?' 'Who are you, Lord?' Saul asked. 'I am Jesus, whom you are persecuting,' he replied. 'Now get up and go into the city, and you will be told what you must do.'"

This encounter with the risen Jesus profoundly changed Saul's life. Struck blind, he was led by his companions into Damascus, where he spent three days without sight, neither eating nor drinking. During this time, Saul experienced a radical transformation in his understanding of Jesus.

God then sent a disciple named Ananias to visit Saul. Despite his initial fear, Ananias obeyed the Lord's instruction. Acts 9:17-18 recounts the moment of Saul's healing and filling with the Holy Spirit:

"Then Ananias went to the house and entered it. Placing his hands on Saul, he said, 'Brother Saul, the Lord—Jesus, who appeared to you on the road as you were coming here—has sent me so that you may see again and be filled with the Holy Spirit.'

Immediately, something like scales fell from Saul's eyes, and he could see again. He got up and was baptized."

This transformative encounter with Jesus fundamentally changed Saul's understanding of the scriptures and his mission. Saul, now Paul, began to see Jesus as the fulfillment of the Law and the Prophets. His deep knowledge of the Old Testament, combined with this new revelation, allowed him to reinterpret the scriptures in the light of Jesus' life, death, and resurrection.

Following his conversion, Paul's initial revelation was that Jesus is the Messiah, the Son of God. Acts 9:20-22 describes his immediate response:

"At once he began to preach in the synagogues that Jesus is the Son of God. All those who heard him were astonished and asked, 'Isn't he the man who raised havoc in Jerusalem among those who call on this name? And hasn't he come here to take them as prisoners to the chief priests?' Yet Saul grew more and more powerful and baffled the Jews living in Damascus by proving that Jesus is the Messiah."

Paul's newfound faith and bold proclamation of Jesus as the Messiah baffled many who knew him as a fierce persecutor of Christians. His dramatic transformation and powerful preaching demonstrated the profound impact of his encounter with Jesus.

Paul's understanding of Jesus as the fulfillment of the scriptures continued to deepen as he spent time in reflection and study. Galatians 1:11-12 and 1:15-17 give us insight into this period of Paul's life:

"I want you to know, brothers and sisters, that the gospel I preached is not of human origin. I did not receive it from any man, nor was I taught it; rather, I received it by revelation from Jesus Christ... But when God, who set me apart from my mother's womb and called me by his grace, was pleased to reveal his Son in me so that I might preach him among the Gentiles, my immediate response was not to consult any human being. I did not go up to Jerusalem to see those who were apostles before I was, but I went into Arabia. Later I returned to Damascus."

During his time in Arabia and Damascus, Paul received further revelation and insight into the gospel. This period of reflection and revelation helped Paul develop a comprehensive understanding of Jesus' fulfillment of the scriptures and the implications of faith righteousness.

To summarize, Paul's dramatic conversion on the road to Damascus marked the beginning of his profound transformation. His encounter with the risen Jesus reshaped his understanding of the scriptures and set him on a mission to proclaim the gospel of Jesus Christ. Paul's deep knowledge of the Old Testament, combined with his revelation of Jesus as the

Messiah, laid the foundation for his teachings on faith righteousness.

In the next lesson, we see Paul's teachings on justification by faith. We will explore key passages in Romans and Galatians to understand how Paul argued that righteousness comes through faith in Jesus Christ, not by adhering to the works of the law.

LESSON 4.2: JUSTIFICATION BY FAITH

In this lesson, we will explore Paul's teachings on justification by faith. This concept is central to Paul's theology and is crucial for understanding the gospel message he proclaimed.

Let's begin by defining what we mean by justification. In theological terms, justification is the act by which God declares a sinner to be righteous on the basis of faith in Jesus Christ. It is a legal declaration, removing the guilt and penalty of sin and attributing righteousness to the believer.

Paul's teachings on justification by faith are most clearly articulated in his letters to the Romans and the Galatians. Let's start with Romans 3:21-26, a key passage where Paul explains the righteousness of God revealed through faith in Jesus Christ:

"But now apart from the law the righteousness of God has been made known, to which the Law and the Prophets testify.

This righteousness is given through faith in Jesus Christ to all who believe. There is no difference between Jew and Gentile, for all have sinned and fall short of the glory of God, and all are justified freely by his grace through the redemption that came by Christ Jesus. God presented Christ as a sacrifice of atonement, through the shedding of his blood—to be received by faith. He did this to demonstrate his righteousness, because in his forbearance he had left the sins committed beforehand unpunished—he did it to demonstrate his righteousness at the present time, so as to be just and the one who justifies those who have faith in Jesus."

In this passage, Paul makes several crucial points:

1. **Righteousness Apart from the Law**: Paul emphasizes that the righteousness of God is revealed apart from the law. This means that it is not based on human effort or adherence to the law but is a gift from God.

2. **Universal Sinfulness**: Paul states that all have sinned and fall short of the glory of God. This universal condition highlights the need for a savior.

3. **Justification by Grace**: Paul explains that justification is a gift of God's grace, received through faith in Jesus Christ. It is not something earned by works but freely given by God.

4. Sacrifice of Atonement: Jesus' sacrificial death is the means by which justification is made possible. Through His shed blood, Jesus atones for sin and satisfies God's righteous requirements.

Paul further elaborates on justification by faith in Romans 4, using Abraham as an example. Let's read Romans 4:1-5:

"What then shall we say that Abraham, our forefather according to the flesh, discovered in this matter? If, in fact, Abraham was justified by works, he had something to boast about—but not before God. What does Scripture say? 'Abraham believed God, and it was credited to him as righteousness.' Now to the one who works, wages are not credited as a gift but as an obligation. However, to the one who does not work but trusts God who justifies the ungodly, their faith is credited as righteousness."

Here, Paul underscores that Abraham's righteousness was credited to him because of his faith, not because of his works. This precedent, established long before the law was given, demonstrates that justification by faith has always been God's plan.

In Galatians 2:15-16, Paul addresses the issue of justification by faith versus works of the law in the context of the early church's struggles with Judaizers, who insisted that Gentile believers must follow Jewish law:

"We who are Jews by birth and not sinful Gentiles know that a person is not justified by the works of the law, but by faith in Jesus Christ. So we, too, have put our faith in Christ Jesus that we may be justified by faith in Christ and not by the works of the law, because by the works of the law no one will be justified."

Paul clearly states that no one can be justified by the works of the law. Justification comes only through faith in Jesus Christ. This message was revolutionary because it opened the way for Gentiles to be included in God's covenant community without having to adhere to the Jewish law.

Let's now consider the implications of justification by faith:

1. **Freedom from the Law**: Believers are no longer under the law's condemnation because they are justified by faith. This freedom means that our relationship with God is not based on our ability to keep the law perfectly but on our trust in Jesus.

2. **Peace with God**: Justification brings peace with God. Romans 5:1 says, "Therefore, since we have been justified through faith, we have peace with God through our Lord Jesus Christ." This peace is a result of our reconciled relationship with God.

3. **Assurance of Salvation**: Justification by faith assures believers of their salvation. Since it is based on God's grace and not on human effort, we can have confidence in our standing before God.

4. **Transformation of Life**: Justification leads to sanctification, the process of becoming more like Christ. While justification is a legal declaration, sanctification is the ongoing work of the Holy Spirit in the believer's life.

To summarize, Paul's teaching on justification by faith is central to his gospel message. It emphasizes that righteousness is a gift from God, received through faith in Jesus Christ, not by works of the law. This doctrine underscores the universal need for a savior, the sufficiency of Christ's sacrifice, and the transformative power of the gospel.

In the next lesson, we will explore the role of the law in revealing sin and our need for a savior. We will see how Paul explains the purpose of the law and its function in leading us to Christ.

LESSON 4.3: THE ROLE OF THE LAW IN REVEALING SIN AND THE NEED FOR A SAVIOR

In this lesson, we will discuss Paul's understanding of the role of the law. According to Paul, the law plays a crucial role in revealing sin and highlighting our need for a savior. By examining key passages in Paul's letters, we will gain a deeper understanding of the purpose of the law and how it leads us to Christ.

Let's begin by considering Paul's statement in Romans 7:7:

"What shall we say, then? Is the law sinful? Certainly not! Nevertheless, I would not have known what sin was had it not been for the law. For I would not have known what coveting really was if the law had not said, 'You shall not covet.'"

Paul makes it clear that the law itself is not sinful. Instead, the law reveals sin by defining what is sinful. The commandment, "You shall not covet," helps us recognize coveting as a sin. Without the law, we would lack a clear understanding of what constitutes sinful behavior.

Paul further explains the purpose of the law in Galatians 3:19-24:

"Why, then, was the law given at all? It was added because of transgressions until the Seed to whom the promise referred had come. The law was given through angels and entrusted to a mediator... Before the coming of this faith, we were held in

custody under the law, locked up until the faith that was to come would be revealed. So the law was our guardian until Christ came that we might be justified by faith. Now that this faith has come, we are no longer under a guardian."

Here, Paul describes the law as a guardian or tutor. The Greek word used, "paidagogos," refers to a tutor or custodian responsible for a child's moral and educational development. The law served this role for the people of Israel, guiding them and revealing their need for a savior. However, once Christ came and faith was revealed, believers were no longer under this guardian.

The law also demonstrates the holiness of God and the seriousness of sin. In Romans 3:20, Paul writes:

"Therefore no one will be declared righteous in God's sight by the works of the law; rather, through the law we become conscious of our sin."

The law's function is not to make us righteous but to make us aware of our sinfulness. By showing us God's holy standards, the law reveals how far we fall short and our inability to achieve righteousness on our own.

Let's consider Romans 5:20-21, where Paul discusses the increase of sin and grace:

"The law was brought in so that the trespass might increase. But where sin increased, grace increased all the more, so that,

just as sin reigned in death, so also grace might reign through righteousness to bring eternal life through Jesus Christ our Lord."

Paul explains that the law causes trespass to increase by making sin more apparent and recognizable. However, this increase in sinfulness highlights the abundance of God's grace. The more we recognize our sin, the more we appreciate the depth of God's grace and the salvation available through Jesus Christ.

In Galatians 3:10-14, Paul contrasts the curse of the law with the blessing of faith:

"For all who rely on the works of the law are under a curse, as it is written: 'Cursed is everyone who does not continue to do everything written in the Book of the Law.' Clearly no one who relies on the law is justified before God, because 'the righteous will live by faith.' The law is not based on faith; on the contrary, it says, 'The person who does these things will live by them.' Christ redeemed us from the curse of the law by becoming a curse for us, for it is written: 'Cursed is everyone who is hung on a pole.' He redeemed us in order that the blessing given to Abraham might come to the Gentiles through Christ Jesus, so that by faith we might receive the promise of the Spirit."

Paul explains that reliance on the works of the law places individuals under a curse because it is impossible to perfectly adhere to all the requirements of the law. The law demands perfect obedience, and failure to meet this standard results in a curse. However, Christ redeemed us from this curse by taking it upon Himself through His sacrificial death. This redemption allows the blessing of Abraham to come to all who have faith in Jesus, both Jews and Gentiles.

In summary, the law serves several critical functions:

1. **Revealing Sin**: The law makes us aware of what constitutes sin and our failure to meet God's holy standards.

2. **Highlighting the Need for a Savior**: By showing us our sinfulness, the law points us to our need for a savior who can provide the righteousness we cannot achieve on our own.

3. **Guiding Us to Christ**: The law acts as a tutor or guardian, leading us to Christ so that we might be justified by faith.

4. **Demonstrating God's Holiness**: The law reveals the holiness of God and the seriousness of sin, emphasizing the need for divine grace and redemption.

Paul's teachings on the law underscore its purpose in God's redemptive plan. The law is not opposed to the promise but works in conjunction with it to reveal our need for Jesus Christ and the justification that comes by faith.

In our next module, we will explore how Paul expounded on these themes in his epistles, particularly in Romans and Galatians. We will see how Paul used his deep understanding of the law and the scriptures to articulate the gospel message and guide the early Christian communities.

MODULE 5:

PAUL'S EXPOSITION OF THE SCRIPTURES IN HIS EPISTLES

In this module, we will explore how Paul expounded on his revelation and understanding of Jesus as the fulfillment of the scriptures in his epistles. Paul's letters to the early Christian communities are rich with theological insights and practical applications that continue to guide believers today.

Paul's deep knowledge of the Jewish scriptures and his profound encounter with the risen Christ equipped him to articulate the gospel message in a way that was both rooted in the Old Testament and relevant to the diverse contexts of the early church. His epistles are a treasure trove of theological exposition, pastoral care, and practical instruction.

In this module, we will focus on three of Paul's key epistles: Romans, Galatians, and Hebrews (though the authorship of Hebrews is debated, its content aligns closely with Pauline theology). We will explore how Paul used these letters to unpack the truths of the gospel and guide the early Christians in their faith.

Here are the main themes we will cover in this module:

1. **Romans – The Gospel of God's Righteousness**:
    o   We will examine the major themes in the book of Romans, including justification by faith, the role of the law, and the righteousness of God. Romans is often considered Paul's magnum opus, providing a comprehensive theological framework for understanding the gospel.

2. **Galatians – The Defense of Faith Righteousness**:
    o   We will delve into Paul's letter to the Galatians, where he passionately defends the gospel of grace against the Judaizers who insisted that Gentile believers must adhere to Jewish law. Galatians is a powerful treatise on the freedom and sufficiency of faith in Christ.

3. Hebrews – The High Priesthood and Sacrifice of Jesus:

o   Though the authorship of Hebrews is debated, its theological depth and focus on the superiority of Christ's priesthood and sacrifice align closely with Pauline thought. We will explore how Hebrews expounds on the fulfillment of the Old Testament sacrificial system in Jesus.

Paul's epistles are not merely theological treatises; they are also pastoral letters written to address specific issues and challenges faced by early Christian communities. By studying these letters, we can gain insights into how Paul applied his theological understanding to real-life situations and provided practical guidance to believers.

As we journey through this module, we will see how Paul's exposition of the scriptures in his epistles reflects his deep conviction that Jesus is the fulfillment of God's redemptive plan. We will explore how Paul's teachings on justification by faith, the role of the law, and the work of the Holy Spirit continue to shape Christian theology and practice today.

Let's begin by diving into the book of Romans, where Paul lays out a comprehensive and systematic presentation of the gospel. We will explore the major themes in Romans and see how Paul uses the Old Testament to support his arguments and illuminate the righteousness of God revealed in Jesus Christ.

LESSON 5.1: ROMANS – THE GOSPEL OF GOD'S RIGHTEOUSNESS

In this lesson, we will delve into the book of Romans, one of Paul's most important and comprehensive epistles. Romans is often considered Paul's magnum opus, providing a systematic presentation of the gospel and its implications for both Jews and Gentiles.

The central theme of Romans is the righteousness of God revealed in the gospel. Paul meticulously outlines how humanity can be justified by faith in Jesus Christ, apart from the works of the law. Let's explore some of the key themes and passages in Romans to understand Paul's theological exposition.

Let's begin with the introduction in Romans 1:16-17, where Paul states the thesis of his letter:

"For I am not ashamed of the gospel, because it is the power of God that brings salvation to everyone who believes: first to the Jew, then to the Gentile. For in the gospel the righteousness of God is revealed—a righteousness that is by faith from first to last, just as it is written: 'The righteous will live by faith.'"

These verses set the stage for the entire letter. Paul declares that the gospel is the power of God for salvation and that it reveals the righteousness of God. This righteousness is received by faith, fulfilling the Old Testament scripture, "The righteous will live by faith" (Habakkuk 2:4).

In Romans 1:18-32, Paul begins by explaining humanity's universal need for salvation. He describes the wrath of God against all ungodliness and unrighteousness. Paul argues that both Gentiles and Jews are under sin and in need of redemption.

Let's move to Romans 3:21-26, where Paul presents the core of his gospel message:

"But now apart from the law the righteousness of God has been made known, to which the Law and the Prophets testify. This righteousness is given through faith in Jesus Christ to all who believe. There is no difference between Jew and Gentile, for all have sinned and fall short of the glory of God, and all are justified freely by his grace through the redemption that came by Christ Jesus. God presented Christ as a sacrifice of atonement, through the shedding of his blood—to be received by faith. He did this to demonstrate his righteousness, because in his forbearance he had left the sins committed beforehand unpunished—he did it to demonstrate his righteousness at the present time, so as to be just and the one who justifies those who have faith in Jesus."

This passage is crucial for understanding Paul's doctrine of justification by faith. Key points include:

1. **Righteousness Apart from the Law**: Paul emphasizes that the righteousness of God is revealed apart from the law. It is a gift of God's grace.

2. **Universal Sinfulness**: Both Jews and Gentiles have sinned and fall short of God's glory, highlighting the need for a universal solution.

3. **Justification by Grace**: Justification is a free gift received by grace through faith in Jesus Christ, not by works of the law.

4. **Atonement through Christ**: Jesus' sacrificial death is the means by which God's righteousness is demonstrated and humanity's sins are atoned for.

Paul continues to elaborate on the implications of justification by faith in Romans 4, using Abraham as an example. Romans 4:1-5 reads:

"What then shall we say that Abraham, our forefather according to the flesh, discovered in this matter? If, in fact, Abraham was justified by works, he had something to boast about—but not before God. What does Scripture say? 'Abraham believed God, and it was credited to him as righteousness.' Now

to the one who works, wages are not credited as a gift but as an obligation. However, to the one who does not work but trusts God who justifies the ungodly, their faith is credited as righteousness."

Paul argues that Abraham's righteousness was credited to him because of his faith, not because of his works. This precedent, established before the law was given, demonstrates that justification by faith has always been God's plan.

In Romans 5:1-2, Paul explains the results of justification by faith:

"Therefore, since we have been justified through faith, we have peace with God through our Lord Jesus Christ, through whom we have gained access by faith into this grace in which we now stand. And we boast in the hope of the glory of God."

Justification by faith brings peace with God, access to God's grace, and the hope of sharing in God's glory. These are profound benefits of the gospel that transform the believer's relationship with God.

In Romans 6, Paul addresses the implications of justification for the believer's life. He explains that justification leads to sanctification, a process of becoming more like Christ. Romans 6:1-4 says:

"What shall we say, then? Shall we go on sinning so that grace may increase? By no means! We are those who have died to sin; how can we live in it any longer? Or don't you know that all of us who were baptized into Christ Jesus were baptized into

his death? We were therefore buried with him through baptism into death in order that, just as Christ was raised from the dead through the glory of the Father, we too may live a new life."

Paul emphasizes that justification by faith does not lead to a life of sin but to a new life in Christ. Believers are united with Christ in his death and resurrection, enabling them to live in righteousness.

In Romans 8, Paul culminates his discussion on the assurance and security of the believer's salvation. Romans 8:1-2 declares:

"Therefore, there is now no condemnation for those who are in Christ Jesus, because through Christ Jesus the law of the Spirit who gives life has set you free from the law of sin and death."

This chapter highlights the transformative power of the Holy Spirit in the believer's life, providing assurance of salvation and freedom from the power of sin and death.

Finally, in Romans 9-11, Paul addresses the relationship between Israel and the Gentiles in God's redemptive plan. He explains that God's promises to Israel are fulfilled in Jesus and that both Jews and Gentiles are included in God's salvation plan through faith.

To summarize, the book of Romans presents a comprehensive and systematic exposition of the gospel. Paul explains how the righteousness of God is revealed in Jesus Christ and received by faith, apart from the works of the law. This gospel brings justification, peace with God, and a transformed life through the power of the Holy Spirit.

In our next lesson, we will explore Paul's letter to the Galatians, where he passionately defends the gospel of grace against the Judaizers who insisted that Gentile believers must adhere to Jewish law. We will see how Paul argues for the freedom and sufficiency of faith in Christ.

LESSON 5.2: GALATIANS – THE DEFENSE OF FAITH RIGHTEOUSNESS

In this lesson, we will explore Paul's letter to the Galatians, where he passionately defends the gospel of grace against those who insisted that Gentile believers must adhere to Jewish law. This letter is a powerful treatise on the freedom and sufficiency of faith in Christ.

The Galatian churches were facing a crisis. Judaizers, who were Jewish Christians insisting that Gentile converts must follow the Mosaic law, particularly circumcision, had infiltrated the church. They argued that faith in Jesus was not enough for salvation; adherence to the law was also necessary. Paul's letter to the Galatians addresses this controversy head-on.

Let's start with Galatians 1:6-9, where Paul expresses his astonishment and concern:

"I am astonished that you are so quickly deserting the one who called you to live in the grace of Christ and are turning to a different gospel—which is really no gospel at all. Evidently some people are throwing you into confusion and are trying to pervert the gospel of Christ. But even if we or an angel from heaven should preach a gospel other than the one we preached to you, let them be under God's curse! As we have already said, so now I say again: If anybody is preaching to you a gospel other than what you accepted, let them be under God's curse!"

Paul's tone is urgent and severe. He emphasizes that the Judaizers' teaching is a perversion of the true gospel. Paul goes so far as to pronounce a curse on anyone, even an angel, who preaches a gospel contrary to the one he preached.

Paul then defends his apostolic authority and the divine origin of his gospel. In Galatians 1:11-12, he writes:

"I want you to know, brothers and sisters, that the gospel I preached is not of human origin. I did not receive it from any man, nor was I taught it; rather, I received it by revelation from Jesus Christ."

Paul asserts that his gospel came directly from Jesus Christ, not from human tradition or instruction. This divine revelation gives his message supreme authority and legitimacy.

In Galatians 2:15-16, Paul articulates the core of his argument for justification by faith:

"We who are Jews by birth and not sinful Gentiles know that a person is not justified by the works of the law, but by faith in Jesus Christ. So we, too, have put our faith in Christ Jesus that we may be justified by faith in Christ and not by the works of the law, because by the works of the law no one will be justified."

Paul emphasizes that even Jews, who had the law, are justified by faith in Christ and not by observing the law. This argument underscores the universality of the gospel—both Jews and Gentiles are justified by faith, not by works.

One of the most famous and powerful passages in Galatians is Galatians 2:20-21, where Paul describes his new identity in Christ:

"I have been crucified with Christ and I no longer live, but Christ lives in me. The life I now live in the body, I live by faith in the Son of God, who loved me and gave himself for me. I do not set aside the grace of God, for if righteousness could be gained through the law, Christ died for nothing!"

Paul's personal testimony here is profound. His old self, defined by adherence to the law, has been crucified with Christ. His new life is lived by faith in Jesus, who loved him and gave Himself for him. Paul insists that if righteousness could be obtained through the law, then Christ's sacrificial death would be meaningless.

In Galatians 3, Paul addresses the role of the law and its relationship to faith. Let's read Galatians 3:10-14:

"For all who rely on the works of the law are under a curse, as it is written: 'Cursed is everyone who does not continue to do everything written in the Book of the Law.' Clearly no one who relies on the law is justified before God, because 'the righteous will live by faith.' The law is not based on faith; on the contrary, it says, 'The person who does these things will live by them.' Christ redeemed us from the curse of the law by becoming a curse for us, for it is written: 'Cursed is everyone who is hung on a pole.' He redeemed us in order that the blessing given to Abraham might come to the Gentiles through Christ Jesus, so that by faith we might receive the promise of the Spirit."

Paul explains that those who rely on the works of the law are under a curse because it is impossible to keep the law perfectly. Instead, righteousness comes through faith, as the scripture says, "The righteous will live by faith." Christ redeemed us from the curse of the law by becoming a curse for us, enabling the blessing of Abraham to come to the Gentiles and allowing us to receive the promise of the Spirit through faith.

Paul further clarifies the purpose of the law in Galatians 3:19-25:

"Why, then, was the law given at all? It was added because of transgressions until the Seed to whom the promise referred had come. The law was given through angels and entrusted to a

mediator. A mediator, however, implies more than one party; but God is one. Is the law, therefore, opposed to the promises of God? Absolutely not! For if a law had been given that could impart life, then righteousness would certainly have come by the law. But Scripture has locked up everything under the control of sin, so that what was promised, being given through faith in Jesus Christ, might be given to those who believe. Before the coming of this faith, we were held in custody under the law, locked up until the faith that was to come would be revealed. So the law was our guardian until Christ came that we might be justified by faith. Now that this faith has come, we are no longer under a guardian."

Paul explains that the law was given because of transgressions, serving as a guardian until Christ came. It was not opposed to God's promises but highlighted humanity's need for a savior. The law's role was to guide and reveal sin, preparing the way for justification by faith in Christ. Now that faith has come, believers are no longer under the guardianship of the law.

Galatians 5:1 emphasizes the freedom that believers have in Christ:

"It is for freedom that Christ has set us free. Stand firm, then, and do not let yourselves be burdened again by a yoke of slavery."

Paul encourages the Galatians to stand firm in their freedom and not to submit again to the yoke of the law. This freedom is not a license to sin but a call to live by the Spirit and in the grace of Christ.

Finally, in Galatians 5:22-25, Paul describes the fruit of the Spirit, which contrasts with the works of the flesh:

"But the fruit of the Spirit is love, joy, peace, forbearance, kindness, goodness, faithfulness, gentleness and self-control. Against such things there is no law. Those who belong to Christ Jesus have crucified the flesh with its passions and desires. Since we live by the Spirit, let us keep in step with the Spirit."

Living by the Spirit produces the fruit of the Spirit, which fulfills the law's righteous requirements. This Spirit-led life is the result of being justified by faith and walking in the freedom Christ provides.

To summarize, Paul's letter to the Galatians is a passionate defense of the gospel of grace. He argues that justification comes through faith in Jesus Christ, not by adhering to the works of the law. This message of freedom and sufficiency of faith is crucial for understanding the true nature of the gospel.

In our next lesson, we will explore the book of Hebrews, focusing on the high priesthood and sacrifice of Jesus. Although the authorship of Hebrews is debated, its content closely aligns with Pauline theology. We will see how Hebrews expounds on the fulfillment of the Old Testament sacrificial system in Jesus.

LESSON 5.3: HEBREWS – THE HIGH PRIESTHOOD AND SACRIFICE OF JESUS

In this lesson, we will explore the book of Hebrews, which, while its authorship is debated, contains profound theological insights that align closely with Pauline thought. Hebrews offers a deep exposition on the high priesthood and the sacrificial work of Jesus, showing how He fulfills and surpasses the Old Testament sacrificial system.

The central theme of Hebrews is the superiority of Christ. The author emphasizes that Jesus is greater than angels, Moses, the Levitical priesthood, and the old covenant sacrifices. This message is particularly relevant to Jewish Christians who were tempted to revert to Judaism to avoid persecution. Let's dive into the key passages that highlight Jesus' high priesthood and His ultimate sacrifice.

Let's begin with Hebrews 1:1-4, which sets the stage for the entire book:

"In the past God spoke to our ancestors through the prophets at many times and in various ways, but in these last days he has spoken to us by his Son, whom he appointed heir of all things, and through whom also he made the universe. The Son is the radiance of God's glory and the exact representation of his being, sustaining all things by his powerful word. After he had provided purification for sins, he sat down at the right hand of the Majesty

in heaven. So he became as much superior to the angels as the name he has inherited is superior to theirs."

This passage introduces Jesus as the ultimate revelation of God, superior to the prophets and angels. It emphasizes His divine nature, His role in creation, and His work of purification for sins. Jesus' exaltation at the right hand of God signifies the completion and sufficiency of His sacrificial work.

Now, let's focus on Hebrews 4:14-16, where the author introduces Jesus as the great high priest:

"Therefore, since we have a great high priest who has ascended into heaven, Jesus the Son of God, let us hold firmly to the faith we profess. For we do not have a high priest who is unable to feel sympathy for our weaknesses, but we have one who has been tempted in every way, just as we are—yet he did not sin. Let us then approach God's throne of grace with confidence, so that we may receive mercy and find grace to help us in our time of need."

These verses highlight Jesus' empathy and sinlessness. As our high priest, Jesus understands our weaknesses and temptations because He experienced them Himself, yet He remained without sin. This dual aspect of empathy and sinlessness qualifies Him uniquely to be our high priest. Because of Jesus, we can approach God's throne with confidence, assured of receiving mercy and grace.

Hebrews 7 further develops the theme of Jesus' high priesthood, contrasting Him with the Levitical priests. Hebrews 7:23-28 states:

"Now there have been many of those priests, since death prevented them from continuing in office; but because Jesus lives forever, he has a permanent priesthood. Therefore he is able to save completely those who come to God through him, because he always lives to intercede for them. Such a high priest truly meets our need—one who is holy, blameless, pure, set apart from sinners, exalted above the heavens. Unlike the other high priests, he does not need to offer sacrifices day after day, first for his own sins, and then for the sins of the people. He sacrificed for their sins once for all when he offered himself. For the law appoints as high priests men in all their weakness; but the oath, which came after the law, appointed the Son, who has been made perfect forever."

Jesus' priesthood is superior because it is eternal and unchangeable. His once-for-all sacrifice is sufficient for all time, unlike the repeated sacrifices of the Levitical priests. Jesus' perfect life and His sacrificial death fulfill and surpass the requirements of the old covenant, providing complete salvation for those who come to God through Him.

Hebrews 8:6-7 introduces the concept of the new covenant, which Jesus mediates:

"But in fact the ministry Jesus has received is as superior to theirs as the covenant of which he is mediator is superior to the old

one, since the new covenant is established on better promises. For if there had been nothing wrong with that first covenant, no place would have been sought for another."

The new covenant, mediated by Jesus, is founded on better promises. It addresses the shortcomings of the old covenant, offering a more profound and lasting relationship with God based on grace and internal transformation rather than external observance.

Hebrews 9:11-14 elaborates on Jesus' high priestly work in the heavenly sanctuary:

"But when Christ came as high priest of the good things that are now already here, he went through the greater and more perfect tabernacle that is not made with human hands, that is to say, is not a part of this creation. He did not enter by means of the blood of goats and calves; but he entered the Most Holy Place once for all by his own blood, thus obtaining eternal redemption. The blood of goats and bulls and the ashes of a heifer sprinkled on those who are ceremonially unclean sanctify them so that they are outwardly clean. How much more, then, will the blood of Christ, who through the eternal Spirit offered himself unblemished to God, cleanse our consciences from acts that lead to death, so that we may serve the living God!"

Jesus' sacrifice is presented in the heavenly sanctuary, which is greater and more perfect than the earthly tabernacle. His blood, unlike the blood of animals, provides eternal redemption and purifies our consciences. This purification enables us to serve the living God with a clean heart and a clear conscience.

Hebrews 10:11-14 emphasizes the finality and sufficiency of Jesus' sacrifice:

"Day after day every priest stands and performs his religious duties; again and again he offers the same sacrifices, which can never take away sins. But when this priest had offered for all time one sacrifice for sins, he sat down at the right hand of God, and since that time he waits for his enemies to be made his footstool. For by one sacrifice he has made perfect forever those who are being made holy."

Jesus' once-for-all sacrifice contrasts with the repetitive and ultimately insufficient sacrifices of the Levitical priests. His sacrifice perfects believers forever, providing complete and lasting atonement. This finality is signified by Jesus sitting down at the right hand of God, indicating that His work of atonement is finished.

The practical implications of Jesus' high priesthood and sacrifice are profound. Hebrews 10:19-23 encourages believers to draw near to God with confidence:

"Therefore, brothers and sisters, since we have confidence to enter the Most Holy Place by the blood of Jesus, by a new and living way opened for us through the curtain, that is, his body, and since we have a great priest over the house of God, let us draw near to God with a sincere heart and with the full

assurance that faith brings, having our hearts sprinkled to cleanse us from a guilty conscience and having our bodies washed with pure water. Let us hold unswervingly to the hope we profess, for he who promised is faithful."

Because of Jesus' sacrifice, we can approach God with a sincere heart and full assurance of faith. Our hearts are cleansed, and we have a secure hope in God's promises. This access to God and the assurance of faith are central to the believer's life.

To summarize, the book of Hebrews presents a compelling exposition of Jesus' high priesthood and His ultimate sacrifice. Jesus is the perfect high priest who offers Himself as the perfect sacrifice, fulfilling and surpassing the old covenant sacrificial system. His once-for-all sacrifice provides complete atonement, eternal redemption, and a purified conscience, enabling believers to draw near to God with confidence.

In our next module, we will explore the practical applications of Paul's teachings for believers today. We will see how the truths of faith righteousness and the fulfillment of the law in Christ can be lived out in our daily lives.

MODULE 6:

PRACTICAL APPLICATIONS FOR BELIEVERS TODAY

In this final module, we will explore the practical applications of Paul's teachings for believers today. Understanding the profound theological truths of faith righteousness and the fulfillment of the law in Christ is essential, but it is equally important to see how these truths can be lived out in our daily lives.

Throughout this course, we have examined Paul's deep insights into the scriptures and his revelation of Jesus as the fulfillment of God's redemptive plan. We have seen how Paul articulated the gospel message in his epistles, emphasizing justification by faith, the role of the law, and the sufficiency of Christ's sacrifice. Now, we turn our focus to how these teachings can transform our lives and guide our walk with God.

In this module, we will explore three main themes:

1. **Understanding Our Identity in Christ**:
   - We will begin by exploring the concept of identity in Christ. Paul teaches that believers are new creations in Christ, and this new identity has profound implications for how we live and relate to God and others. We will examine key passages that highlight our identity as children of God, heirs with Christ, and members of the body of Christ.

2. **Living Out Faith Righteousness in Daily Life**:
   - We will delve into the practical outworking of faith righteousness. Justification by faith not only changes our legal standing before God but also transforms our daily lives. We will explore how faith righteousness leads to a life characterized by love, holiness, and good works, reflecting the character of Christ in all we do.

3. **The Role of the Old Testament in Christian Faith**:
   o Finally, we will consider the ongoing relevance of the Old Testament for believers today. While we are no longer under the law as a means of justification, the Old Testament remains a vital part of God's revelation. We will discuss how to read and apply the Old Testament in light of the fulfillment of the law in Christ, seeing its value for instruction, encouragement, and spiritual growth.

Paul's teachings are not merely abstract doctrines; they are transformative truths meant to be lived out in the real world. In Ephesians 4:1, Paul urges believers to "live a life worthy of the calling you have received." This module will help us understand what it means to live out our calling as followers of Jesus, grounded in the truths of the gospel.

As we journey through this final module, we will see how the foundational truths we have studied can shape our character, guide our decisions, and empower us to live faithfully in a complex and challenging world. The gospel is not only the power of God for salvation but also the power for living a transformed life.

Let's begin by exploring our identity in Christ and seeing how this new identity forms the basis for our life and conduct as believers.

LESSON 6.1: UNDERSTANDING OUR IDENTITY IN CHRIST

In this lesson, we will explore the concept of our identity in Christ. Understanding who we are in Christ is foundational to living out the Christian life. Paul's epistles provide profound insights into our new identity as believers, highlighting the transformative power of the gospel.

Let's begin by considering 2 Corinthians 5:17, where Paul succinctly describes our new identity in Christ:

"Therefore, if anyone is in Christ, the new creation has come: The old has gone, the new is here!"

This verse emphasizes that being in Christ makes us new creations. Our old identity, defined by sin and separation from God, is gone. We are now new creations, transformed by our relationship with Jesus. This new identity is the basis for our relationship with God and how we live our lives.

In Ephesians 1:3-14, Paul outlines several aspects of our identity in Christ. Let's read through this passage and highlight key points:

"Praise be to the God and Father of our Lord Jesus Christ, who has blessed us in the heavenly realms with every spiritual

blessing in Christ. For he chose us in him before the creation of the world to be holy and blameless in his sight. In love he predestined us for adoption to sonship through Jesus Christ, in accordance with his pleasure and will—to the praise of his glorious grace, which he has freely given us in the One he loves. In him we have redemption through his blood, the forgiveness of sins, in accordance with the riches of God's grace that he lavished on us. With all wisdom and understanding, he made known to us the mystery of his will according to his good pleasure, which he purposed in Christ, to be put into effect when the times reach their fulfillment—to bring unity to all things in heaven and on earth under Christ.

In him we were also chosen, having been predestined according to the plan of him who works out everything in conformity with the purpose of his will, in order that we, who were the first to put our hope in Christ, might be for the praise of his glory. And you also were included in Christ when you heard the message of truth, the gospel of your salvation. When you believed, you were marked in him with a seal, the promised Holy Spirit, who is a deposit guaranteeing our inheritance until the redemption of those who are God's possession—to the praise of his glory."

This passage highlights several key aspects of our identity in Christ:

1. **Blessed with Every Spiritual Blessing**: We are richly blessed in Christ with every spiritual blessing in the heavenly realms.

2. **Chosen and Predestined**: God chose us in Christ before the creation of the world to be holy and blameless. We are predestined for adoption as sons and daughters through Jesus Christ.

3. **Redeemed and Forgiven**: In Christ, we have redemption through His blood and the forgiveness of sins, according to the riches of God's grace.

4. **Recipients of God's Wisdom and Understanding**: God has made known to us the mystery of His will, purposing to bring unity to all things in Christ.

5. **Included and Sealed with the Holy Spirit**: When we believed, we were included in Christ and marked with the Holy Spirit, guaranteeing our inheritance.

These truths about our identity in Christ are transformative. They assure us of God's love and purpose for our lives, providing a foundation for how we live and relate to others.

In Galatians 3:26-29, Paul emphasizes our identity as children of God and heirs of the promise:

"So in Christ Jesus you are all children of God through faith, for all of you who were baptized into Christ have clothed yourselves with Christ. There is neither Jew nor Gentile, neither

slave nor free, nor is there male and female, for you are all one in Christ Jesus. If you belong to Christ, then you are Abraham's seed, and heirs according to the promise."

Paul highlights that our faith in Christ makes us children of God. This new identity transcends ethnic, social, and gender distinctions, uniting us as one in Christ. As heirs of the promise given to Abraham, we are part of God's covenant family.

Another key aspect of our identity in Christ is our membership in the body of Christ. In 1 Corinthians 12:12-13, Paul explains:

"Just as a body, though one, has many parts, but all its many parts form one body, so it is with Christ. For we were all baptized by one Spirit so as to form one body—whether Jews or Gentiles, slave or free—and we were all given the one Spirit to drink."

Being in Christ means we are part of a larger community—the body of Christ. Each believer is a vital member of this body, with unique gifts and roles. This communal identity calls us to live in unity and serve one another.

Paul also emphasizes our identity as citizens of heaven. In Philippians 3:20-21, he writes:

"But our citizenship is in heaven. And we eagerly await a Savior from there, the Lord Jesus Christ, who, by the power that enables him to bring everything under his control, will transform our lowly bodies so that they will be like his glorious body."

As citizens of heaven, our ultimate allegiance is to God's kingdom. This heavenly citizenship shapes our values, priorities, and hope. We look forward to the return of Christ and the transformation of our bodies to be like His glorious body.

Understanding our identity in Christ is foundational for living out the Christian life. It assures us of God's love and purpose, unites us with other believers, and shapes our values and priorities. This new identity empowers us to live confidently and faithfully, reflecting the character of Christ in all we do.

In our next lesson, we will explore how faith righteousness transforms our daily lives. We will examine how justification by faith leads to a life characterized by love, holiness, and good works.

LESSON 6.2: LIVING OUT FAITH RIGHTEOUSNESS IN DAILY LIFE

In this lesson, we will explore how faith righteousness transforms our daily lives. Understanding justification by faith is essential, but it is equally important to see how this truth impacts our behavior, relationships, and priorities. Paul's epistles provide practical guidance on living out the implications of our faith righteousness.

Let's begin by considering Galatians 5:16-18, where Paul explains the role of the Holy Spirit in guiding our lives:

"So I say, walk by the Spirit, and you will not gratify the desires of the flesh. For the flesh desires what is contrary to the Spirit, and the Spirit what is contrary to the flesh. They are in conflict with each other, so that you are not to do whatever you want. But if you are led by the Spirit, you are not under the law."

Paul emphasizes that living out our faith righteousness involves walking by the Spirit. The Holy Spirit empowers us to overcome the desires of the flesh and live in a way that pleases God. This Spirit-led life is characterized by a daily dependence on God's guidance and strength.

In Galatians 5:22-23, Paul describes the fruit of the Spirit, which reflects the character of Christ in our lives:

"But the fruit of the Spirit is love, joy, peace, forbearance, kindness, goodness, faithfulness, gentleness and self-control. Against such things there is no law."

The fruit of the Spirit encompasses qualities that should be evident in the life of every believer. These characteristics are the natural outgrowth of a life led by the Spirit and aligned with God's will. They reflect the transformation that occurs when we live out our faith righteousness.

Let's consider how these qualities can be lived out in our daily lives:

1. **Love**: As followers of Christ, we are called to love others selflessly. In 1 Corinthians 13, Paul provides a detailed description of love, highlighting its patience, kindness, and selflessness. Living out love means putting others' needs above our own and seeking their well-being.

2. **Joy**: Joy is a deep-seated sense of well-being and contentment that comes from knowing God. It is not dependent on circumstances but is rooted in our relationship with Christ. Living out joy involves maintaining a positive attitude and finding reasons to rejoice, even in difficult times.

3. **Peace**: Peace is the absence of conflict and the presence of harmony. It involves trusting God and experiencing His calm in the midst of life's challenges. Living out peace means being peacemakers, resolving conflicts, and promoting reconciliation.

4. **Forbearance (Patience)**: Patience involves enduring difficult situations and people with a calm and forgiving spirit. It means being slow to

anger and quick to forgive. Living out patience requires relying on God's strength to endure and respond graciously.

5. **Kindness and Goodness**: Kindness and goodness involve treating others with compassion and integrity. They reflect a heart that seeks to do good and bless others. Living out kindness and goodness means being proactive in helping and serving those around us.

6. **Faithfulness**: Faithfulness is being reliable and trustworthy. It means keeping our commitments and being steadfast in our faith. Living out faithfulness involves being dependable in our relationships and consistent in our walk with God.

7. **Gentleness**: Gentleness involves being considerate and tender in our interactions with others. It means being strong yet controlled in our responses. Living out gentleness requires treating others with respect and sensitivity.

8. **Self-Control**: Self-control involves managing our desires and impulses in a way that honors God. It means exercising discipline and restraint. Living out self-control requires relying on the Holy Spirit to help us make wise and godly choices.

In addition to the fruit of the Spirit, Paul provides practical instructions on living out our faith righteousness in various aspects of life. Let's look at Romans 12:1-2, where Paul calls believers to live sacrificially and renew their minds:

"Therefore, I urge you, brothers and sisters, in view of God's mercy, to offer your bodies as a living sacrifice, holy and pleasing to God—this is your true and proper worship. Do not conform to the pattern of this world, but be transformed by the renewing of your mind. Then you will be able to test and approve what God's will is—his good, pleasing and perfect will."

Paul urges us to offer our bodies as living sacrifices, dedicating our entire lives to God as an act of worship. This involves resisting the patterns of the world and allowing God to transform our minds through His Word. Living out faith righteousness means aligning our thoughts, attitudes, and actions with God's will.

In Colossians 3:12-17, Paul provides further guidance on how to live out our new identity in Christ:

"Therefore, as God's chosen people, holy and dearly loved, clothe yourselves with compassion, kindness, humility, gentleness and patience. Bear with each other and forgive one another if any of you has a grievance against someone. Forgive as the Lord forgave you. And over all these virtues put on love, which binds them all together in perfect unity. Let the peace of Christ rule in your hearts, since as members of one body you were called to

peace. And be thankful. Let the message of Christ dwell among you richly as you teach and admonish one another with all wisdom through psalms, hymns, and songs from the Spirit, singing to God with gratitude in your hearts. And whatever you do, whether in word or deed, do it all in the name of the Lord Jesus, giving thanks to God the Father through him."

Paul instructs us to clothe ourselves with virtues that reflect Christ's character. These include compassion, kindness, humility, gentleness, and patience. Forgiveness and love are paramount, as they promote unity and peace within the body of Christ. Additionally, Paul emphasizes the importance of gratitude and letting the message of Christ dwell richly among us, shaping our interactions and worship.

In summary, living out faith righteousness involves allowing the Holy Spirit to produce His fruit in our lives, offering ourselves as living sacrifices, and clothing ourselves with Christ-like virtues. These actions reflect the transformation that occurs when we embrace our new identity in Christ and live according to the gospel.

In our next lesson, we will explore the role of the Old Testament in the life of a believer today. We will discuss how to read and apply the Old Testament in light of the fulfillment of the law in Christ, seeing its value for instruction, encouragement, and spiritual growth.

LESSON 6.3: THE ROLE OF THE OLD TESTAMENT IN CHRISTIAN FAITH

In this lesson, we will explore the role of the Old Testament in the life of a believer today. Understanding how to read and apply the Old Testament in light of the fulfillment of the law in Christ is essential for our spiritual growth and understanding of God's redemptive plan.

The Old Testament is a rich and vital part of God's revelation. It provides the foundation for the New Testament and is integral to the full narrative of Scripture. Jesus Himself affirmed the importance of the Old Testament. In Matthew 5:17-18, He said:

"Do not think that I have come to abolish the Law or the Prophets; I have not come to abolish them but to fulfill them. For truly I tell you, until heaven and earth disappear, not the smallest letter, not the least stroke of a pen, will by any means disappear from the Law until everything is accomplished."

Jesus makes it clear that He came to fulfill the Old Testament, not to abolish it. The Old Testament points to Christ and finds its fulfillment in Him. Therefore, it remains relevant and valuable for us today. Let's explore how we can read and apply the Old Testament as Christians.

First, let's consider the instructional value of the Old Testament. In 2 Timothy 3:16-17, Paul writes:

"All Scripture is God-breathed and is useful for teaching, rebuking, correcting and training in righteousness, so that the servant of God may be thoroughly equipped for every good work."

When Paul wrote this, the Scriptures he referred to were primarily the Old Testament. The Old Testament is divinely inspired and useful for teaching, rebuking, correcting, and training in righteousness. It equips us for every good work by providing wisdom, moral guidance, and spiritual insights.

Let's look at some specific ways the Old Testament can be applied in our lives today:

1. **Understanding God's Character and Attributes**:
   o The Old Testament reveals much about God's character and attributes, such as His holiness, justice, mercy, and faithfulness. For example, in Exodus 34:6-7, God describes Himself to Moses:

2. *"And he passed in front of Moses, proclaiming, 'The Lord, the Lord, the compassionate and gracious God, slow to anger, abounding in love and faithfulness, maintaining love to thousands, and forgiving wickedness, rebellion and sin. Yet he does not leave the guilty unpunished; he punishes the children and their children for the sin of the parents to the third and fourth generation.'"*

o   This passage helps us understand the balance of God's mercy and justice. Reflecting on these attributes deepens our worship and trust in God.

3. Learning from Biblical History and Examples:

o   The Old Testament is filled with historical narratives and examples that offer lessons for our faith and conduct. In 1 Corinthians 10:11, Paul writes:

4.   *"These things happened to them as examples and were written down as warnings for us, on whom the culmination of the ages has come."*

o   Stories of figures like Abraham, Moses, David, and the prophets provide valuable lessons in faith, obedience, and perseverance. They also serve as warnings against disobedience and unbelief.

5. Understanding God's Redemptive Plan:

o   The Old Testament lays the foundation for understanding God's redemptive plan, culminating in Jesus Christ. Prophecies, types, and foreshadows in the Old Testament point to Christ and His work of salvation. For example, the sacrificial system described in Leviticus foreshadows Jesus' ultimate sacrifice for sin.

6. Moral and Ethical Guidance:

o The Old Testament provides moral and ethical guidance that remains relevant. The Ten Commandments (Exodus 20:1-17) and wisdom literature, such as Proverbs, offer principles for righteous living. While some specific laws were given to Israel under the old covenant, their underlying principles often have timeless application.

Next, let's discuss how to read the Old Testament in light of its fulfillment in Christ. Jesus' life, death, and resurrection fulfill the Old Testament prophecies, types, and laws. This fulfillment means that while the Old Testament remains valuable, we must interpret it through the lens of Christ.

1. Christ-Centered Reading:

o Approach the Old Testament with a focus on how it points to Christ. For example, when reading about the Passover lamb in Exodus 12, consider how it prefigures Jesus as the Lamb of God who takes away the sin of the world (John 1:29).

2. **Understanding the Continuity and Discontinuity**:
    o   Recognize what continues and what has been transformed by Christ. For instance, the moral principles of the Old Testament (e.g., love your neighbor) continue to apply, while the ceremonial laws (e.g., animal sacrifices) have been fulfilled in Christ's sacrifice.

3. **Application to Christian Life**:
    o   Apply Old Testament teachings in a way that aligns with New Testament revelation. For example, the call to justice and mercy in Micah 6:8 is reinforced by Jesus' teaching on loving your neighbor as yourself (Matthew 22:39).

In conclusion, the Old Testament remains a vital part of God's revelation, offering instruction, examples, and insights into His character and redemptive plan. Reading it through the lens of its fulfillment in Christ enriches our understanding and application of its teachings.

As we wrap up this course, let's reflect on how Paul's revelation of Jesus as the Lamb of God and his teachings on faith righteousness have deepened our understanding of the gospel and its implications for our lives. Thank you for joining me in this exploration. May the truths we've studied transform our lives and draw us closer to Christ.

COURSE CONCLUSION:

PAUL'S REVELATION OF JESUS AS THE LAMB OF GOD AND FAITH RIGHTEOUSNESS ROOTED IN SCRIPTURE

As we come to the end of our journey through Paul's profound teachings and the rich tapestry of scripture, let's take a moment to reflect on what we've learned and how it can transform our lives.

Throughout this course, we have explored Paul's deep understanding of the Old Testament and his revelation of Jesus Christ as the fulfillment of God's redemptive plan. We have seen how Paul's teachings on faith righteousness, justification by faith, and the role of the law provide a comprehensive framework for understanding the gospel.

Let's recap the key themes and insights from each module:

1. **Paul's Background and Scriptural Foundation**:
   o We examined Paul's background as a Pharisee and his deep knowledge of the Jewish scriptures. This foundation helped us understand how Paul's revelation of Jesus as the Messiah was rooted in his study of the Old Testament.

2. **The Sacrificial System and the Promise of a Redeemer**:
   o We explored the Old Testament sacrificial system and the story of Abraham and Isaac, seeing how these pointed to the need for a perfect sacrifice. Paul recognized Jesus as the ultimate fulfillment of these types and shadows.

3. **Jesus as the Fulfillment of the Old Testament**:
   o We delved into Jesus' own teachings on fulfilling the Law and the Prophets, and how He saw Himself as the culmination of God's promises. Paul's writings consistently reflect this understanding.

4. **Paul's Revelation and Teachings on Faith Righteousness**:

   o We studied Paul's conversion and his teachings on justification by faith. Paul's epistles, especially Romans and Galatians, articulate the transformative power of faith in Jesus Christ.

5. **Paul's Exposition of the Scriptures in His Epistles**:

   o We examined how Paul used his deep knowledge of the Old Testament to explain and defend the gospel in his letters. We focused on Romans, Galatians, and Hebrews, seeing how Paul's theological insights were applied to the early Christian communities.

6. **Practical Applications for Believers Today**:

   o We explored the practical implications of Paul's teachings for our lives today. Understanding our identity in Christ, living out faith righteousness, and reading the Old Testament in light of its fulfillment in Christ are crucial for our spiritual growth.

Paul's revelation and teachings offer a profound and transformative understanding of the gospel. By grasping the depth of Paul's insights, we can appreciate the continuity of God's redemptive plan and the sufficiency of Christ's work on our behalf. This understanding equips us to live faithfully and boldly as followers of Jesus.

As we conclude, let's consider how we can continue to apply these truths in our daily lives:

1. **Deepen Your Study of Scripture**:
   - Continue to study both the Old and New Testaments, looking for the connections and fulfillment in Christ. Allow the Holy Spirit to guide you into deeper understanding and application of God's Word.

2. **Embrace Your Identity in Christ**:
   - Live out your identity as a new creation in Christ. Let your understanding of who you are in Him shape your actions, relationships, and priorities.

3. **Walk by the Spirit**:
   - Rely on the Holy Spirit to produce His fruit in your life. Seek to be led by the Spirit in all areas, allowing Him to transform you into the image of Christ.

4. **Live Out Faith Righteousness**:
   - Reflect the righteousness you have received by faith in your daily conduct. Demonstrate

love, kindness, patience, and all the fruit of the Spirit in your interactions with others.

5. **Value the Old Testament**:

   o Continue to read and value the Old Testament as part of God's revelation. See it as foundational to understanding the full narrative of Scripture and God's redemptive work.

Thank you for joining me on this journey through Paul's revelation of Jesus as the Lamb of God and faith righteousness rooted in scripture. I hope this course has deepened your understanding and strengthened your faith. May the truths we have studied continue to transform your life and draw you closer to our Savior, Jesus Christ.

Pray with me.

Heavenly Father, we thank You for the incredible gift of Your Word and the profound truths revealed through Your servant Paul. Thank You for sending Your Son, Jesus, to fulfill the law and the prophets and to bring us into a relationship with You through faith. Help us to live out our identity in Christ, walk by the Spirit, and reflect Your love and righteousness in all we do. Guide us as we continue to study Your Word and apply it to our lives. In Jesus' name, we pray. Amen.

Thank you once again for participating in this course. God bless you as you continue to grow in your faith and live out the gospel.

ABOUT THE AUTHOR

Clint Byars is the founding and lead pastor of Forward Church in Sharpsburg, GA. He has authored 8 books and published over 100 teaching series. Clint created a series of prayer and meditation resources titled Tools for Transformation. Clint's current project building Forward School of Transformation with courses and transformational journeys.

Clint has a practical yet profound teaching style that focuses on the New Covenant identity and authority of the believer. "I believe that when you experience God's love, you will allow him to transform you."

Clint graduated from Impact International School of Ministries, founded by Dr. Jim Richards, where he served as a youth pastor, outreach director, and ministry school instructor. Clint is also a regular guest speaker at Charis Bible College in Woodland Park, Colorado, founded by Andrew Wommack.

You can access hundreds of free resources at clintbyars.com. We recommend becoming a monthly Resource Member, where you can download ALL of Clint's teachings, meditations, and eBooks and also get course discounts.

ADDITIONAL RESOURCES

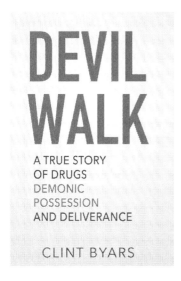

TOOLS FOR TRANSFORMATION

Mind-renewal is crucial to experience lasting transformation. I have developed tools that use Biblical wisdom and modern technology to equip you in putting on your true identity in Christ.

— Clint Byars - creator of Tools for Transformation

Jesus said "ALL things are possible for those who believe." I want to help you BELIEVE so all of His promises become possibilities in your life. Prayer and meditation WILL produce transformation if you engage your heart in the process, I can show you how.

Meditation and Prayer are not magic, they do not force God's hand or mystically manifest your desires. Prayer and meditation simply make God's promises believable. God's word WILL multiply in a receptive heart. I can show you how to prepare your heart and plant God's Word. The seed of His Word will do the rest.

Transformation is the final frontier for the Jesus follower. Everything you want to see happen in your life will manifest through renewing your mind and believing God's promises. The transformation and success you desire will not come through behavioral modification or law-keeping, it comes as you harmonize with your true eternal spiritual identity and outwardly reflect the indwelling spirit of God.

JOSHUA 1:8 Keep this Book of the Law (instruction) always on your lips; meditate on it day and night, so that you may be careful to do everything written in it. Then you will be prosperous and successful.

My Tools for Transformation will teach you how to cultivate God's Word in your inner man to facilitates belief in your heart. When you believe from your heart, you will no longer hinder His kingdom from manifesting in your life. Truly, all things are possible for those who believe. My Tools for Transformation will equip you to persuade your heart to BELIEVE.

Visit www.toolsfortransformation.me for more about these revolutionary resources.

FORWARD SCHOOL OF TRANSFORMATION

PERSONAL GROWTH

Invest in yourself. Take the time to establish your heart in your New Creation identity in Christ. You will experience personal transformation which will empower you to succeed as well as walk out your calling.

BECOME EQUIPPED

As you experience transformation, your inner man will become more receptive to God's leading in your life. God has a plan for you, He has assignments for you, we can equip you to fulfill those assignments and see God's will established in your life.

ENRICHMENT

Personal transformation and equipping in the ministry of reconciliation are vital for personal success and fulfilling God's call on your life. As you launch out, it is important to continue to invest in yourself and enrich your understanding.

Visit www.forwardschooloftransformation.com for a FREE Discipleship course, as well as more courses to help you establish your heart in grace and become equipped in the ministry of reconciliation.

FEATURED COURSES

- Discipleship Foundations
- Who Do You Love?
- Ephesians and Colossians

Made in the USA
Columbia, SC
13 September 2024